THE LUXURY TRAVELER'S HANDBOOK

Liberating luxury for the smart traveler.

Sarah & Terry Lee

The Luxury Traveler's Handbook: Liberating luxury for the smart traveler.

© Copyright 2012 by Sarah & Terry Lee

ISBN 978-1-927557-00-6

All rights reserved. No part of this publication may be reproduced, stored in or introduced into a retrieval system, or transmitted in any form or by any means (electronic, mechanical, photocopying, recording or otherwise), without the prior written permission of both the copyright owner(s) and the above publisher of the book.

ISBN 978-1-927557-00-6

Cataloguing data available from Library and Archives Canada

Disclaimer:

This book provides entertaining and informative snapshots of the writers' personal experiences and helpful tips from the writers and others, learned while traveling around the world. The tips provided in this book are not meant to serve as an exclusive checklist to effectively safeguard the reader in every travel situation. Each reader should complete updated, detailed research from legitimate sources to learn the cultural norms and safety recommendations for their specific destination. No one can guarantee safety and travel can expose everyone to potential risks. Because safety is impacted by each person's actions and choices, each reader is advised to always do their homework on their destination and use their best judgment while on their journey.

We wish you safe, happy and luxurious travels.

Terry:
*To my mum Mya, whose wise counsel keeps me grounded,
and my dad Tommy, whose wanderlust I inherited.*

Sarah:
To my mother Margery, whose belief in me ensures I believe in myself.

Acknowledgements

We've so many people to thank for their assistance in writing *The Luxury Traveler's Handbook*. But first, we'd like to thank ourselves for not killing each other during the more stressful parts of the writing and editing process.

Our gratitude goes to Janice Waugh, the inspiration behind the Traveler's Handbook series, for her shrewd guidance and endless patience. Thank you to Jeff Jung, Jodi Ettenberg and Shannon O'Donnell for providing detailed and acutely perceptive insights which substantially enhanced the book. The camaraderie of Janice, Jeff, Jodi, and Shannon has provided vital levity and unfailing support during the creative process.

Grateful thanks to Elena Paschinger, our wonderful Austrian friend who speedily read our drafts. She showed true friendship and devotion, and enriched the book with astute observation and comment.

We are indebted to Sarah's brother, Warren Davis whose forensic attention to detail greatly aided our early drafts. Thanks for your insights.

Thank you to Tracey Nesbitt and Ana Botelho, whose skill and professionalism are only matched by their patience.

And last, but by no means least, a huge thank you to our readers at LiveShareTravel.com whose encouragement and support give us the strength to put up with airport security pat downs and keep on traveling

Contents

Liberating Luxury 5
- Liberating Luxury for Your Travels 6
- Our Appetite for Luxury Travel 10
- What Does Luxury Travel Mean to You? 11
- Putting Luxury on the List 12

Dream Trips to Real Trips 13
- Plan Your Escape 14
- Seven Hot and Affordable Luxury Destinations 14
- The Luxury Travel Landscape and Liberate Luxury Tips 16
- Budgeting for Your Trip 36
- Getting There: Choose Your Class 38
- Finding the Best Luxury Deals 42
- Meet the Agent 43
- Package Your Own Vacation 44
- Our 12-Point Plan to Packaging Your Vacation and Finding the Best Deals Online ... 45
- Great Prices Gone in a Flash 51
- Benefit from Your Loyalty 54
- Our 12-Point Plan to Loyalty Programs 55
- Feel the Fear and Do It Anyway 58

Living Luxury 65
- Seven Hot Trends in Luxury Travel 67
- Get Packing 68
- It's About the Journey 70
- How to Get an Upgrade 73
- A Stylish Stay – Hotels and Cruises 75
- The Star System 77
- A Luxury Service 81
- Choose Your Luxury Experience 84
- Stepping Out into the Real World 87

Contents

Playing it Safe..93
Words to the Wise: Consumer Rights..94
Avoiding Travel Scams..95
Is Luxury Travel Safe? 97
Seven Ways to Keep You and Your Belongings Safe.................98
Watch What You Eat: Tasty Tips...102

Go in Style 103
More Luxury, More Choice 104

Resources 107

Endnotes 118

Luxury Travel Stories
Our Back Story... 1
Now That's What We Call Luxury 8
Christmas Past and Future... 22
"Can a wellness clinic make me a new man?"........................... 28
The Rockies Revealed... 35
How to Save $4,650 in 11 Days 48
Parking to Check-In 72
Five Luxury Mysteries.. 79
An Ayurvedic Adventure 85
Sarah's Bangkok 90
A Phantom Menace?... 100

Our Back Story

We enjoy a little luxury on our travels. It has become central to how we venture forth across the world.

We revel in its finery, in the sumptuousness of its comfort. But we also delight in getting luxury for less.

Added to that, we never let luxury stand in the way of us and the reasons why we travel – to have real experiences and meet real people.

We first met in Terry's office on one of those dull, damp days that we in England lovingly refer to as summer. Glancing out the window at the incessant rain we excitedly exchanged tales of lands far away.

> ❖❖ *We've seen the world without it costing the Earth.* ❖❖

We had both traveled fairly widely – Sarah since she was just a few months old when her mom took her on the first of many trips to Barbados. She continued traveling through her youth including spending three months in Romania while at university. Terry had been to a number of interesting places including historic lands like Israel and some countries that no longer existed, such as Yugoslavia and East Germany. But there was still much that we wanted to see, so many places that tickled our travel taste buds. Destinations rolled off our tongues with tantalizing ease. There was passion between us, our lust was wanderlust.

Like most people we held regular jobs. Sarah was a journalist and later managing editor of travel magazines. Terry worked in communications and policy in local government, hoping to make a difference for the community. We weren't rich, just fairly comfortable.

But with an endless appetite for travel, we made good use of our vacation time. Our first trip was a traditional package to the Greek island of Zakynthos and while it was beautiful, the accommodation was poor. We decided there and then that just having a place to rest was not good enough. We wanted comfort, quality accommodation – yes, we wanted some luxury.

In the past ten years we've visited fifty countries and uncovered many ways to get value from our luxury travels. From the Americas, to Asia, Africa, the Middle East and all across Europe, we've taken everything from weekend breaks to month-long tours. We've enjoyed beach vacations and cruises, city breaks and mountain escapes, all while staying in a range of luxury accommodation. We even used our knowledge to arrange our wedding in Thailand and put together our guests' trips.

For us, travel has been a marriage of thrilling adventures, enthralling experiences and stylish stays. In this book we share our experiences and the insider tips we've unearthed to help you discover luxury travel without breaking the bank.

In 2010 we launched *LiveShareTravel* (LiveShareTravel.com), an online travel and lifestyle magazine aimed at helping readers find luxury for less with news, features, tips and reviews. We've traveled extensively, highlighting some of the best value-for-money luxury experiences around.

We've seen the world without it costing the Earth. Now we'll show you how to do it.

Taking time out from our luxury stay in Koh Samui, Thailand, to join in with *Songkran* (Thai New Year) festivities. Yes, that's two giant water cannons on the day bed before us.

Sarah & Terry Lee

LIBERATING LUXURY

"As I've grown older I've needed more stars in my hotels."

Anon

Liberating Luxury for Your Travels

Comfort is all well and good, but who doesn't enjoy a little luxury?

Rich, elegant, desirable – luxury is a luscious, coveted pleasure.

In travel, the concept of luxury takes on even greater meaning, placing many travelers beyond the boundaries of their everyday existence. Luxury is the difference between arriving refreshed after a comfortable flight or stiff from being bent-double in a cramped seat. It is the difference between entering your hotel room knowing you'll feel at home and walking in comforting yourself that "it's only a place to sleep."

There's a sense with luxury travel that it's exclusive – even elitist – and unattainable to people on anything but a celebrity budget. But luxury travel doesn't have to be costly.

Expensive may be reassuring to some. But many of us feel more reassured, even thrilled, by the prospect of getting luxury for less. This is a philosophy we share, especially in the prevailing economic climate when even those with executive incomes have reassessed their travel arrangements, cutting back on lavish vacations.

In straitened economic times, with people working harder and longer, and with the impact this has on family life, we believe people should enjoy the very best of travel. Instead of lowering standards it's time to travel smarter. The purpose of this book is to make luxury travel accessible – we're liberating luxury for the smart traveler.

Luxury shouldn't be reserved solely for that once-in-a-lifetime dream vacation, and we intend to show you how to get value for money on every trip.

We know that it's possible because we have achieved it. We've liberated luxury to make our upscale travels possible on an average income. And we've done so while having countless exciting, eye-opening, culturally enlightening, and personally empowering experiences.

In this book, you'll find information on everything from flights to accommodation, cruises and travel extras. From package deals to do-it-yourself vacations, flash sales to loyalty programs, we'll help you find great luxury travel deals.

We'll also explore trip planning, demystify star ratings, explain your rights as a consumer, and discuss how to enjoy your luxury break in safety.

Naturally, luxury travel will rarely come with a budget price tag. To keep a realistic grip on budget and still deliver luxury experiences, we'll concentrate on the middle to high end of the luxury travel bracket – think premium economy flights and four-star hotels upwards.

But most of all, we want to make your money travel as far as you do.

Now That's What We Call Luxury

We bobbed beneath an inky sky, suspended in the salt water. Watching stars punctuate the night with their glow, we felt privileged. Not because we were at one of the most secluded hotels in India, but because staying there allowed us an opportunity to gaze upon what was, to us, a little-known world.

Traveling to this distant shore we had discovered a place cut-off from the light pollution of the 21st century. Strangely, despite the excellent service, elegant accommodation and fine cuisine, proffered by the most attentive staff, we felt insignificant. But then, the universe has a way of keeping you grounded.

India isn't the only place where we've experienced luxury travel and the luxury of travel. We've been left in a state of bliss after being scrubbed, wrapped and massaged at some of the best resorts in the Caribbean, and at chic chalets amid the fresh air of Austria's mountain peaks.

> *Luxury travel is about more than plumped pillows, posh resorts, and decadent dining. It's a feeling.*

We've stayed in hotels on exotic beaches in Asia, where it wasn't enough that our villa was a mere ten feet from the waves that lapped the shore – we also had to bypass our own swimming pool, day beds and hammock to get to it. We've eaten at fine restaurants on land and at sea, aboard some fabulous cruise ships.

But luxury travel is about more than plumped pillows, posh resorts and decadent dining. It's a feeling.

It's the buzz we got after setting out from our hotel in Cape Town, South Africa. Driving the Cape Peninsula, we struck out on our own, discovering beautiful beaches and the wilds of the rugged landscape.

It's the fascination of sharing the same hotel as movie star Michael Caine in Da Nang, Vietnam, and later spotting locations we'd visited in his latest film.

It's the joy of feasting our eyes on the peerless beauty of the Caribbean Sea, off the coast of Mexico, while sailing on a private yacht for the day.

It's the thrill we gain from our adventures – watching giraffe through the panoramic window of our safari lodge, or soaring over Victoria Falls by helicopter.

It's the fulfillment of experiencing different cultures and visiting famous landmarks such as the White House in Washington, the Colosseum in Rome, and the Louvre in Paris.

Luxury travel offers us much, leaving us feeling treated, excited, and ready for more.

Visiting beautiful natural and man-made sights like Milan's Duomo in Italy, are among the attractions of luxury travel for us.

Our Appetite for Luxury Travel

We all travel according to our personal preference or budgetary limitations, but few of us choose to rough it. Today, even hostels are catering to people who want a little more luxury with boutique-style offerings such as California king-sized beds, en-suite bathrooms, and designer furniture.

Then there's a newer breed of traveler: the flashpacker. Though traveling with a backpack, flashpackers want to stay somewhere providing every convenience, and with style in abundance.

And it doesn't end there. In the past, camping was more the preserve of Scouts than of luxury travelers. But it has undergone a renaissance with "glamping," or glamorous camping, taking off in diverse locations.

You're not alone in your love of luxury. This sector of travel has grown considerably in the past twenty years. There are an estimated 200,000 luxury rooms, in 200 destinations around the world.[1] And there are an increasing number of magazines, websites, and tour companies dedicated to elegant escapes.

Some think luxury travel doesn't allow for a real experience. They question how you can get under the skin of a destination, particularly in a developing country, while peering through the rose-tinted window of a five-star resort.

For us luxury and a real experience are not mutually exclusive: a hotel or resort is a place for us to rest and rejuvenate, and a first class flight simply a way to travel more comfortably. As long as you're interested in discovering more about your destination – and most travelers have a natural curiosity about the world – luxury shouldn't dictate the depths of your cultural immersion.

What Does Luxury Travel Mean to You?

Encompassing a multitude of experiences, luxury travel always offers you more: more comfort, more space, more service, more options, and more indulgences. All of which can leave you feeling special, pampered, and relaxed.

For us it's not just about a first-rate journey to our destination, or spending time in quality accommodation. It's also about the location we stay in, and the individual care and attention we receive.

Throughout *The Luxury Traveler's Handbook*, travelers, writers, and industry professionals will share their views. But what does luxury travel mean to you?

We urge you to consider your definition:

- What do you want from your luxury vacation?
- How do you want it to make you feel?
- How important are the individual aspects of luxury travel to you – from transportation to accommodation, setting and experiences?

Understanding what defines the luxury experience for you will help when it comes to planning your next escape.

❝ *When I think of luxury the first words that come to mind are comfort, choice, and ambience. Any one of these components may be present on different occasions but to have them all present in one place is delightful. Another defining concept is the idea of the non-essential. To have the option of non-essential qualities of comfort and enjoyment is an extra special gift. Finally, luxury represents a degree of excellence beyond the ordinary and is therefore something to be valued and desired.* ❞

Sandy Brudenall, luxury traveler

Putting Luxury on the List

Identifying your definition of luxury and listing your requirements is a great place to start, but let us tickle your palate with some travel operators recognized for excelling in the provision of luxury.

In 2012 Condé Nast Traveler magazine celebrated its 25th anniversary by announcing a Platinum Circle of hotels and cruise lines which made its Gold List[2] in each of the last five years. While the Condé Nast Traveler Platinum Circle is divided by region, we have gone through the list to highlight the total highest overall scores (bracketed numbers denote tied position):

1. Four Seasons, Sharm el Sheikh, Egypt[3]

2. Kirawira Luxury Tented Camp, Serengeti National Park, Tanzania[4]

3. Mandarin Oriental Hotel, Bangkok, Thailand[5]

4. Mombo and Little Mombo Camps, Moremi Game Reserve, Botswana[6]

(4). Oberoi Udaivilas, Udaipur, India[7]

(4). One&Only Palmilla, San Jose del Cabo, Mexico[8]

7. Hôtel de Paris, Monte Carlo, Monaco[9]

8. Pudong Shangri-La, Shanghai, China[10]

(8). Londolozi Game Reserve, Sabi Sand Game Reserve, South Africa[11]

(8). Singita Sabi Sand, Sabi Sand Game Reserve, South Africa[12]

These awards reveal that some of the best luxury experiences can be found in the least expected destinations. You'll find them in the wilds of an African safari reserve or in the heart of Asia's bustling cities – something we'll pick up on in the next section.

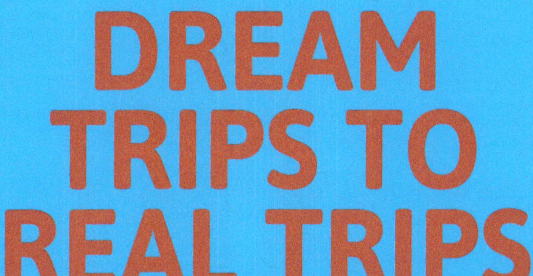

DREAM TRIPS TO REAL TRIPS

" Throw your dreams into space like a kite and you do not know what it will bring back, a new life, a new friend, a new love, a new country."

Anaïs Nin

Plan Your Escape

So far we've made no mention of budgets – we'll get to that shortly. But it's important to dream first and explore the options available. After all, visualizing a vacation is part of the joy of travel. It's also the key to deciding what you want to do and, most importantly, where you'd like to go.

There are countless opportunities for the luxury traveler, but let's consider some destinations that are hot right now.

Seven Hot and Affordable Luxury Destinations

The luxury traveler's taste is forever changing as traditionally strong destinations reveal new hotels or attractions and lesser-known regions come to the fore. These destinations are currently well and truly en vogue:

- **Costa Rica** is pulling in a growing number of visitors eager to experience its pristine rainforests and unique ecosystems. This green corner of Latin America – Costa Rica is one of the most bio-diverse countries on Earth – is seeing more and more boutique and upscale hotels opening, as well as fractional developments (upscale, shared ownership properties).

- **Croatia** has long been popular for its cozy coastal hideaways and glut of impressive designer hotels, while cosmopolitan capital Zagreb and Dubrovnik are seeing increasing numbers of visitors. Dubrovnik's Old Town, a popular port of call on cruise itineraries, is worthy of a longer stay to soak up its history and dine at sophisticated eateries like Nautika – lauded as one of the most romantic restaurants in the world.

- **Thailand's** various sights and attractively priced luxury hotels are well documented, but neighbors Vietnam and Cambodia are giving it a run for its money. In Vietnam, serious value can be found in Hoi An, Halong Bay, Da Nang, Nha Trang and Hue, with five-star hotels averaging $140 per night. In Cambodia you will find eastern luxury for less at the highly-rated Siem Reap art deco hotel, The Privilege Floor, with rates starting at approximately $180.[13]

- **St Vincent and the Grenadines** earned the dubious accolade for the most expensive all-inclusive resort in the Caribbean. The Buccament Bay Resort averages $1,482 per night for a double room in high season.[14] But don't let this put you off. This island chain is shaping up to be the next tropical haven with plenty of reasonably-priced four- and five-star hotels.

- **Colombia** certainly appeals to the luxury traveler looking for an off-the-beaten-track experience, and boutique or eco-hotels. The country's reputation and image have been boosted by improved security and significantly reduced crime rates. Its landscapes range from dense jungles to snow-capped mountains to gorgeous beaches. Then there's Cartagena, where smart boutique hotels have become as popular as the salsa played in the city's bars. Other attractions include the Rosario Islands, which sit like rosary beads in the Caribbean Sea, and the iconic city of Medellín.

- **Brazil** has it all, from exciting beachside cities to the deep jungle of the Amazon. It appeals to eco-conscious luxury travelers, due to its excellent sustainable resorts. Paraty, hailed as the most culturally rich destination in the Costa Verde – the 325-mile coastline between Rio de Janeiro and São Paulo – is also proving popular. Photography, music and literary festivals attract the likes of Ian McEwan, Isabel Allende and Salman Rushdie. Paraty is also set for French chic with a Relais & Châteaux hotel about to open there.

- **Greece's Costa Navarino** in the Peloponnese region, where sandy beaches lead into the inviting waters of the Ionian Sea, is one of Europe's hot hideaways. Just a few years old in tourism terms, Costa Navarino already hosts luxury stalwarts like The Westin, while a Banyan Tree – Europe's first resort where all accommodation is villa-based and each has its own pool - is also set for the region. There are also stylish boutique options in towns like Monemvasia (monemvasia.com), a delightful medieval castle city in the southern Peloponnese.

> " *For me, it all boils down to the 'three sigh test' of relaxation. If I manage to sigh on three separate occasions, I can truly say I'm in a place of luxury. That feeling when you look out on a stunning view and sigh deeply in awe of the sight. Or when you finish an incredible bottle of Pomerol. Or when you finally lie down on a Hästens bed and sigh in relaxation. Three sighs are quite tough to achieve - but it is possible. Regardless of the current global downturn, travelers are still looking for luxury experiences. The only difference now is that it has to be worth it in respect to their perception of value-for-money.* "

Nathalie Salas, of PerfectBoutiqueHotel.com

The Luxury Travel Landscape and Liberate Luxury Tips

Once upon a time luxury travel amounted to stays at hotels like The Ritz, cruising on a fine ocean liner or taking a journey by rail on opulent routes like the Orient Express. But as our appetites for travel have grown, so too have the varieties of ways in which luxury lovers discover vacations that suit their travel personalities.

Here we explore the luxury travel landscape to help you find the vacation that's right for you.

Look out for our Liberate Luxury tips to get the best from each.

Destination: Hotel

There was a time when a hotel was just a place to lodge. Then, the "destination hotel" checked in – hotels and resorts at the heart of the vacation experience. Their facilities are so plentiful and varied that they don't need to be close to a tourist destination to attract visitors, and you don't feel the need to leave your accommodation.

Many of the Caribbean's all-inclusive resorts like those of the Sandals and Bahía Principe brands offer such luxury. Similarly the Atlantis hotels in The Bahamas and Dubai, fall into this category and have the largest open-air marine habitats in the world alongside water parks, spas and entertainment centers.

Glitzy Dubai is also home to Burj Al Arab, which comes into the destination hotel bracket as an "address hotel" – one so famous for quality, elegance and indulgence that it has become synonymous with luxury. The very names of these legendary hotels - The Savoy in London, The Plaza in New York, or Raffles in Singapore - encapsulate refinement, and that alone attracts guests. All are landmarks renowned for unrivaled service, heritage, and luxury on a grand scale.

Burj Al Arab is a relative address hotel newcomer, having opened in 1999, but it has quickly become a destination in itself. It has sumptuous suites, public areas featuring the world's tallest atrium, rare Italian marble, and 2,000 square meters of 24-carat gold leaf.

Liberate Luxury:

Book a destination hotel in low season. If you're staying for the hotel itself, the weather and other factors are of little consequence. Burj Al Arab is one of the world's most expensive hotels, but it offers enormous discounts at the height of Dubai's steamy summers.

Visit Burj Al Arab in Dubai's steamy summer months and secure serious discounts.

The Beauty of Boutique Hotels

City breaks were long epitomized by stays at address hotels and businesslike chains such as Intercontinental, Hilton, and Sheraton. They attracted guests with excellent service and brand consistency. But fast on their heels came a younger, sexier breed of luxury city hotels and the trend soon spread beyond urban areas.

Boutique hotels aren't a new phenomenon, but they have grown in popularity since their debut in New York in 1984[15] by promising guests something larger brands can't: a unique and strong identity, usually characterized by design-led interiors, localized and unusual features. Part of the quirky nature of boutique hotels is that they fit their surroundings, be it the "too cool for school" Harajuku district of Tokyo, the Haussmann grace of a Parisian boulevard, or the laid-back boardwalks of Cape Cod. They also feel comfortably small or medium-sized and are rarely traditional in style.

There are boutique brands such as Small Luxury Hotels of the World, Red Carnation, and Morgans Hotels. Major chains also offer boutique chic, such as Starwood's W Hotels. But many boutique hotels are independent operations. Facilities, quality and service can vary widely so it's always best to do your research and check a variety of online reviews before booking.

Liberate Luxury:
Flash sale companies, which offer deals for short periods of time, love boutique hotels and offer some pretty good rates if you're flexible about dates and destination.

Live Like a Stylish Local

There has been a growing trend in luxury travel which we call "socially-sourced" accommodation. It involves individuals listing rental properties, or even leasing their own homes when they travel, through a network of online agents like Airbnb, Roomorama, HouseTrip and Wimdu.

Claiming to be the world's first "unhotel," onefinestay (onefinestay.com) allows you to stay in one of 350 luxury homes in Central London, while homeowners are on vacation. Among the properties in its portfolio are the largest boat on the River Thames and a palatial home in stately Knightsbridge.

Liberate Luxury:
If you like the comforts of home and enjoy staying in less touristy locations, socially-sourced accommodation could work for you, giving you a real, local experience.

Life of Luxury – Vacation Ownership

Timeshare: Since the 1960s, timeshare has offered people the chance to vacation at four- and five-star resorts around the world, for the rest of their lives, for a one-time investment.

It became an increasingly popular way to travel, and largely in luxury, but the public's knowledge and understanding of it faded over time. For example, few people realize that you can exchange your timeshare to visit other resorts worldwide through companies like RCI and Dial An Exchange. In addition, it garnered a bad reputation in the 1980s and 90s, mostly due to high pressure sales techniques, rather than the product itself.[16]

Fractional: If timeshare is generally graced with quality resorts, an even more luxurious form of shared ownership – the umbrella term for this type of accommodation – is fractional. A fractional property can amount to a condo-hotel: apartments in hotel blocks that owners can rent out, a destination club or a private residence club. They are typically located in sought-after destinations, feature exceptionally spacious accommodation, high quality fixtures and fittings, and plenty of extra services like lifestyle concierges.

As a deeded property, fractional shares can be sold, with the owner cashing in on any equity. It also allows buyers to purchase according to the amount of time that they can spend in a property and they are usually sold in units of from four to thirteen weeks.

Like timeshare, fractional ownership comes with ongoing maintenance fees. However, it's a fraction of the cost of maintaining a second home abroad.

Luxury brands like Hilton, Marriott, Disney, Four Seasons, Fairmont, and Ritz-Carlton all have a shared ownership arm to their businesses. It is also possible to buy fractional shares of yachts and private jets.

Liberate Luxury:

Book a timeshare or fractional property vacation to try it out. Most companies want you to sample their product, and offer very inexpensive rates. Timeshare rentals also offer good value, as resorts will rent accommodation that is not being used by owners at low cost. You can book directly with resorts or via websites like Endless Vacation Rentals.

Gran Meliá Palacio de Isora, one of the most glamorous timeshare resorts in Tenerife in the Canary Islands – a haven for European timeshare owners.

Christmas Past and Future

There's nothing quite like knowing that you're assured of quality when you reach your accommodation.

As we arrived for a pre-Christmas break at our fractional villa at Arcos Gardens in the heart of Andalucía, we knew we were in for a treat. After all, quality is the benchmark of a fractional property.

> 66 *The marching drew ever closer until we found ourselves surrounded by Roman centurions.* 99

Our five-bedroom villa was newly-built and accessorized with modern designer fixtures, including a SieMatic kitchen, Gaggenau appliances, a Bang & Olufsen sound system and home cinema. Heading outside we found our private swimming pool glistening in the midday sun, and we immediately made plans to watch the sunset from our hot tub while enjoying a bottle of Rioja.

Later that evening we left the reassuring newness of our villa behind to visit the nearby town of Arcos de la Frontera, which dates back to the 13th century. Our shoes clicking against the cobbled streets, we wandered uphill past centuries-old buildings, drawn into the heart of the town by the sound of music and marching feet.

Arcos de la Frontera was celebrating one of its biggest annual festivals. Performed just before Christmas, *Belén Viviente* (Living Nativity) sees the townsfolk re-enact scenes from one of the oldest stories in the world.

The sound of marching drew ever closer until we found ourselves surrounded by Roman centurions. In one home King Herod's court was in full swing, with belly dancers performing for the King and onlookers. In a courtyard the Three Wise Men prepared to follow the star, and in a nearby stable Mary cradled a real-life baby Jesus while Joseph looked on proudly.

Above: Mary cradles the baby Jesus in a centuries-old festival in Arcos de la Frontera, Spain.
Below: The height of modernity – our Arcos Gardens villa.

Vie for Villas

Once only affordable by the rich and famous, luxury villas are now within the budgets of most people traveling in a group. Found the world over, villas are available with designer furnishings, swimming pools, saunas, whirlpools, maid, butler, chef and concierge services. As villas can sleep large numbers of people, the price per person is usually attractive, allowing a family or a group of friends to experience luxury for less than the price of a four- or five-star hotel.

Villas are available for rent through individuals and small companies as well as large brands. Luxury travel company Abercrombie & Kent offers villas in Europe and the Caribbean. In Barbados, you can also find them in the much sought-after Sandy Lane Estate. There are even luxury resorts that provide private villas which include access to all the amenities of the resort.

Liberate Luxury:
Ask for a discount on villa rates as there is always room for negotiation.

Luxury as a Family Affair

A stylish hotel may seem too stuffy a location for children, but the luxury family market is growing. Hotels worldwide are accommodating them with more than just kids' clubs – some even have children's spas.

Luxury Family Hotels is a chain of noble properties in the United Kingdom, including The Ickworth Hotel in Suffolk, which is set amid the grandeur of a former country estate. The company caters to children with magical fairy gardens, in-room baby monitors, daycare, older children's clubs, garden play equipment and room types suitable for families with three children or more.

Beaches Resorts are renowned for all-inclusive Caribbean family vacations offering Kids Camps, Xbox 360 Game Garages and DJ Academies, as well as activities such as sailing, windsurfing and snorkeling. In the evenings, clubs serve non-alcoholic cocktails in a parent-free zone.

Liberate Luxury:
Parents can benefit from loyalty programs. Some, like Hyatt, offer extras for families such as a second room for children at half price.

The Rotunda is the centre piece of the historic Ickworth Hotel in Suffolk, UK. Its gardens are a great place for children to play.

Sustainable Style

As concerns about the environment grew there was a move towards developing green, sustainable travel options. Unfortunately, some of the accommodations were a far cry from luxurious.

Today there is plenty of choice, innovation and quality for the green luxury traveler. Eco-conscious hospitality companies worldwide are embracing luxury – often tying the two qualities together in quaint boutique hotels or glamorous yurts – thereby liberating green travelers to see the planet while minimizing their environmental impact.

Some will argue that hotels merely pay lip service to green issues as part of their marketing efforts, but as companies realize that going green is good business, more are joining this quiet environmental revolution. In Lake Tahoe, California, 968 Park Spa Resort is one of those using eco-friendly, sustainable materials and processes, and featuring locally-sourced food.[17] The all-suite five-star Hacienda Tres Ríos in the Riviera Maya, Mexico, was built from the ground up to stringent environmental guidelines, and partners with non-profit agencies to offer socially and culturally enlightening tours.

Liberate Luxury:

Give back by joining a hotel "voluntourism" program. These can be environmental, perhaps helping save sea turtles, or social, such as programs run by Ritz-Carlton or Sandals Resorts, which fund schools in the Caribbean.

The Luxury of Wellness

Wellness is becoming synonymous with luxury trips and can run the gamut from holistic yoga breaks, to pampering at the world's most renowned hotels, to cosmetic surgery, medical advice and dentistry.

More than just treatments and gym workouts, wellness can encompass the complete resort experience – including rooms, beds, food, ambience, and décor – all designed to help you de-stress, and return your sense of wellbeing.

As they say at St. Lucia's The BodyHoliday, Le Sport: "Give us your body for a week and we'll give you back your mind".[18]

The array of treatments available at spa and wellness resorts are too numerous to mention and range from the deliciously sublime to the creative and, at times, bizarre – nightingale excrement facial, anyone? But most offer treatments, fitness programs, saunas and steam baths.

You can even plan your travels around a wellness theme by visiting hotels or whole regions specializing in ancient therapies like ayurveda, balneotherapy or thalassotherapy.

Liberate Luxury:

While access to spa facilities and gyms is usually free at hotels, treatments can be expensive. Seek out deals with free treatments or all-inclusive wellness packages.

There are many ways to enjoy a relaxing spa experience and in Seefeld, Austria, you can bathe in beer - it's certainly different.

"Can a wellness clinic make me a new man?" Asks Terry

As a man of the Midlands in England, I wasn't especially open to alternative therapies. So when I was invited to stay at the SHA Wellness Clinic I felt a long way from home.

The term "wellness clinic" suggested hallways thick with the smell of disinfectant, medical types in white coats and dormitory beds with lights out by 9:30 p.m.

I hurried to the hotel's website. It described its philosophy of helping guests care for mind and body through a combination of ancient oriental techniques and advanced western medicine, re-establishing a harmonious balance between body, mind and spirit.[19] Nothing too bad about that, I thought, but remained to be fully convinced.

Stepping out of the taxi I was taken by the freshness in the air. The SHA is set on a hill near the town of Villa de Altea, Alicante, in Spain, with panoramic views across the region.

> 66 *That evening, I was intrigued to be served a macrobiotic dinner. I'd heard of macro photography and macroeconomics but wasn't sure I wanted macros in my dinner.* 99

The first thing that struck me was that the staff weren't wearing white coats, although you could find one or two in the clinic area. There I also found a huge menu of treatments and procedures from cellular stimulation to focalized ultrasounds and sleep recovery. Many of these things left me bemused. I'm sure these features suited the hotel's celebrity guests like Gwyneth Paltrow, Kylie Minogue and Naomi Campbell. But what could it offer a chap like me?

Still, the views from the SHA impressed me and my room was stunning, with a huge terrace and hot tub. I had no trouble relaxing.

That evening I was intrigued to be served a macrobiotic dinner. I'd heard of macro photography and macroeconomics but wasn't sure I wanted macros in my dinner.

Macrobiotic cooking, I discovered, utilizes organic products, based on the suggestions of nutritionists.[20] The meal was surprisingly delicious and I savored every dish including rare tuna, mixed vegetables, and chocolate coolant with ginger ice-cream. It made me think that if healthy food was always this good, I'd eat it more often.

When it came time to leave I did so reluctantly. The hotel had won me over with its light and airy design, wonderful food and focus on health and well-being. I was totally relaxed. Would I say that I left the SHA Wellness Clinic a new man? Perhaps not. But I did feel more open to the possibilities of what a wellness clinic could offer, even to a Midlands boy like me.

Glam Up the Great Outdoors

There was a time when camping was as glamorous as a monkey in stilettos. Then glamping arrived.

Whether you call it glamorous, cool or posh camping, glampsites, as they're known, are cropping up all over the world. They give us a chance to take in the great outdoors – glampers love getting close to nature – without compromising on style and comfort.

A typical glampsite is like a hotel with fabulous outdoor access. They have eco-friendly designer tents or yurts connected to power and water supplies and are furnished with conveniences from crisp linens, to hot tubs, and more.

Amid the lush green jungle of the Cambodian-Thai border, 4 Rivers Floating Lodge is the world's first floating luxury tent resort. It's accessible only by boat and its tents are linked by floating walkways as are the bar, gourmet restaurant and library. The tents have Wi-Fi and DVD players and there's an array of boat trips and jungle treks to choose from.

The glacial valley of Minaret Station, in New Zealand, has a luxury tented camp accessible only by helicopter. Guests stay in tented suites complete with sheepskin carpets, king-sized beds, en-suite facilities and private decks with their own hot tubs.

Liberate Luxury:
Do your research. As glamorous as the accommodation may be, not all glampsites have en-suite bathroom facilities.

Luxury on an Ocean Wave

There was a time when cruising was said to be the preserve of the newly-wed and the nearly dead, but those days are certainly over. Cruising is undergoing a renaissance with a huge number of ships ordered in the past five years and, as of June 2012, another 53 scheduled for delivery by 2016.[21]

Preparing for dinner – the glamorous main dining room aboard Celebrity Cruises' Equinox.

Ships range from river cruisers to small ocean-going towns with up to 6,000 passengers. Many of today's larger ships provide excellent entertainment, endless facilities and staterooms, or cabins, through to plush penthouses.

But there's yet another level of cruise elegance available. Smaller ships, with approximately 1,000 passengers, are perfecting luxury with butler and concierge services, all-inclusive packages and all-balcony suites.

> *Liberate Luxury:*
> Few cruises are all-inclusive (though meals are usually covered) so look out for special offers when booking, such as free onboard credit or free excursions.

Charter Your Yacht

Luxury yachts aren't solely for the extraordinarily rich and fabulously famous. Whether you're an experienced sailor or a total novice, there's a sailing vacation to suit you.

Yachts are available for charter everywhere from New York to the Pacific Islands and you can book a single cabin or charter your own yacht with a small group. Either way, it allows for some independence and impromptu stops for a dip in the ocean or a call ashore.

Larger, crew-manned yachts can have spas, and a wide choice of water sports such as scuba diving, waterskiing, kayaking and jet-skiing.

Around the world yachting comes in different forms, from Turkish gulets to 50-foot Discovery catamarans in the wilds of Scotland, and oak-paneled houseboats in South Africa.

> *Liberate Luxury:*
> Whole yacht charters, particularly with a crew, are rarely a cheap option. But, as with villas, chartering a larger vessel for a group can be very economical.

Elegance on the Rails

Luxury train travel offers a world of style and glamor as you take in international vistas that linger in the memory. These are a far cry from everyday national train services and can include fine dining, butler service, and even spas.

Here is a sample of some of the best rail experiences around the world:

Europe: Spain's El Transcantábrico Clasico runs between León and Santiago de Compostela, an eight-day journey through the country's northern towns and villages. Stopping each evening, it provides an opportunity to enjoy local nightlife and a good night's sleep.

The legendary Orient Express, which ran from 1883-2009, is the epitome of our romance with the rails. Though the original service no longer operates, a version of it – the Venice Simplon-Orient-Express - now runs popular routes through numerous European countries, while the Orient-Express' Royal Scotsman cuts across Scotland and northern England.

South America: Orient-Express offers one of the world's most incredible journeys aboard the Hiram Bingham from Cusco to the base of Machu Picchu in Peru. Passengers can watch the landscape unfold from Pullman carriages furnished in 1920s style.

Asia: Orient-Express' Eastern & Oriental Express takes in Singapore, Malaysia, Thailand and Laos. In India, the Maharajas' Express runs a series of regal routes from Bangalore to Rajasthan, and the Golden Triangle of Delhi, Jaipur and Agra on trains like the Deccan Odyssey and the Palace on Wheels.

Africa: Rovos Rail runs a stylish route from Cape Town to Durban, Pretoria, Victoria Falls, Etosha National Park, the Kalahari Desert, Namibia's capital of Windhoek, and Dar es Salaam, in Tanzania. South Africa's other slice of luxury on the rails is the Blue Train where guests enjoy exquisite cuisine and the best of South African wines.

Australasia: Great Southern Rail operates four trains across Australia from coast to coast. The Ghan, The Overland, Indian Pacific and The Southern Spirit offer a Gold Service with compact sleeper accommodation, stylish restaurant car, a lounge car and cabin steward service. They also have private carriages accommodating up to eight people with fully-equipped kitchens, private dining rooms and chefs.

Liberate Luxury:

Few of these trains are low-cost options, but with prices including accommodation, meals, and travel through plenty of regions/countries, it can be a good all-inclusive deal as well as a great experience.

The Rockies Revealed, by Terry

"All aboaaaaard!" shouted the station master. The train whistled as if in response to the whoops of encouragement from staff lining the platform of Vancouver's Rocky Mountaineer Station.

Wanderlust and anticipation coursed through me as I climbed aboard the world renowned Rocky Mountaineer for a train journey through Canada's immense Rocky Mountains.

> *I secretly would have loved to have slept onboard – right there, in my seat, under the stars that filled the glass roof at night.*

I had chosen the GoldLeaf Service, which tantalized with luxury in the form of a glass-domed roof – for 180-degree views of the mountain vistas – and gourmet meals on the lower deck.

Over the next four days we journeyed 280 miles a day through the lush green of Vancouver to the Rockies' snow-capped peaks. Delighting in my plush carriage I looked up, thrilled to see the roof filled with views of precipitous mountains racing heavenwards.

Next we trundled through the arid desert of Kamloops before journeying onwards to the beguiling beauty of Banff. Each night we alighted from the train to stay in local hotels, affording us a few hours to experience the towns. I must admit, I secretly would have loved to have slept onboard – right there, in my seat, under the stars that filled the glass roof at night. There I would have completely immersed myself in the glorious Canadian scenery and this iconic journey.

Budgeting for Your Trip

You might be planning the trip of a lifetime but you don't want to pay for it for the rest of your life.

Having a budget for a vacation is important. It establishes the parameters of what you can do and where you can go. It also acts as a restraint for those who might get carried away. Ultimately, deciding what to spend your money on and where to stretch the budget is a choice influenced by personal preference. Here are some common-sense considerations:

- Think about where you'll benefit most from extra luxury. Is it in your flight, a hotel, or on attractions in your destination? It's worth investing in the comfort of upgraded seats on a 20-hour flight to Australia, but as we'll explore, business class is rarely worth the investment on short flights.

- Don't leave vacation planning too late. It's important to have enough time to seek out the best deals and stretch your travel dollar. The days of rock-bottom last minute deals are now largely over.

- Carry out initial research on the price per night of accommodation in your destination so that you will have a guide to the costs you may expect.

- Identify your big ticket travel essentials. Planning your "must-haves" will give you a better sense of budget.

- Take a little more spending money than you anticipate needing. Your budget for extras will be determined by your destination, board basis (i.e. bed and breakfast through to all-inclusive) and what you want to do on vacation. As the New York Times' Susan Heller said: "When preparing to travel, lay out all your clothes and all your money. Then take half the clothes and twice the money."[22]

- Don't forget to budget for tips for porters, tour guides and more. They can really add up.

Whirling dervish show after a desert safari, in Sharjah, United Arab Emirates. Budgeting for your trip will ensure you can afford plenty of extras.

Getting There: Choose Your Class

Luxury accommodation is all very well but surely the journey should be as comfortable and enjoyable as time spent in your destination.

Most airlines operate on a price and quality structure. Beyond the normal coach class there are three levels of travel to choose from: premium economy, business and first class.

On a long-haul flight, usually anything from four hours upwards, comfort is a major consideration. However, the difference in pricing between coach, premium economy, business, and particularly first class can be huge and the expenditure difficult to justify.

Take, for example, a 12-hour return flight from London to Bangkok. On any given day the prices can change, but on one check (June 2012) we found the following rates:

Coach	British Airways: $1,436	Thai Airways: $1,334
First class	British Airways: $8,363	Thai Airways: $6,487

For many it will be difficult to justify the thousands of dollars price difference when booking a first class seat. This is especially true when, for a fraction of that amount, you could upgrade to premium economy, book into five-star accommodation for the duration of your vacation, and still have change.

But what do you get for your money?

Premium Economy

Premium economy is becoming increasingly popular with passengers aiming to upgrade from the cramped conditions of coach without having to make the giant leap to vastly more expensive business and first class. It has also become one of the most profitable sections of a plane, making it popular with airlines. They tempt passengers with comfort: increased seat pitch (or extra legroom), up to two inches extra seat width, up to three inches greater reclining capacity, adjustable headrests, leg rests and lumbar support. They also offer extra baggage allowances, larger personal television screens, premium refreshments, and amenity kits with eye masks, socks and toiletries.

Airline review site SeatGuru.com suggests that when the extra cost of premium economy is 10-15 percent more than coach, it represents good value for the comfort-conscious flier.

If you book in advance, premium economy is approximately 85 percent more expensive than a coach fare for flights across the Atlantic Ocean (USA to Europe and vice versa). This can drop to as low as 10 percent, as coach fares tend to be substantially higher the closer you get to departure date.[23] So it's worth remembering to ask about premium fares if you have a last minute coach flight booking.

Keep an eye out for day-of-travel upgrades. If an airline hasn't filled their premium seats, it can offer discounted upgrades at check-in.

Business Class

Business class is on average 65 percent more expensive than premium economy,[24] but is literally a class apart in terms of space and amenities, with up to 50 percent more legroom, significantly greater recline, more substantial leg rests and headrests, and superior food and wine service.

On short-haul flights you'll find business class offers minor improvements over coach, such as no middle seat, two inches extra seat width, up to seven inches of extra legroom and complimentary food and drinks. Long-haul business class, however, can offer the following upgrades:

- double the seat pitch (legroom) of coach
- two to three extra inches of seat width compared to coach
- more degrees of recline
- electric seat controls to adjust recline position, leg rest and lumbar support
- larger personal TV screens and more viewing options
- laptop power ports

- premium food and wine service
- increased cabin staff to passenger ratio
- amenity kits including socks, eye masks and toiletries.

First Class

First class on long-haul flights is in a completely different league in luxury travel. For example, Virgin Atlantic has had bars on board for many years for what it calls its Upper Class passengers. On today's superjumbo jets – Airbus A380s – first class passengers are treated to everything from massages to showers and double-bedded suites.

But generally, first class passengers flying long-haul can expect to find:

- ten to thirty extra inches of seat pitch (legroom) compared to business class
- one to two extra inches of seat width compared to business class
- more degrees of recline over business class seats
- electric seat controls to adjust recline position, leg rest and lumbar support
- larger personal TV screens and more viewing options
- laptop power ports
- premium food and wine service
- more privacy due to smaller cabin size
- increased cabin staff to passenger ratio
- amenity kits including pajamas, slippers, eye masks and toiletries.

While in-flight amenities, service and entertainment in business and first class are often comparable across airline carriers, the type of seat offered can vary significantly. These fall into the categories of recliner seats, lie-flat seats, flat bed seats, and suites and are described by SeatGuru.com as:

Recliner Seats: These provide excellent space and comfort but do not have the significant recline of lie-flat and flat bed seats.

Lie-Flat Seats: While airlines often market these as having up to 180 degrees of recline, they are slightly angled and do not lay completely flat. Passengers often find these seats extremely comfortable for relaxing and working, but not conducive to sleep when in the fully-reclined position because of the awkward angle.

Flat Bed Seats: When fully reclined, these seats are completely horizontal, creating a bed that is fully flat. They regularly receive accolades for comfort as seats and beds.

Suites: Offering the utmost in privacy and comfort, each suite is essentially its own mini-cabin with a fully-flat bed, work station and television.[25]

What's in a Name?

Always bear in mind that airlines can give different names to the same type of cabin class; for example, British Airways' World Traveler Plus is premium economy, the same cabin as Delta's Economy Comfort and Air France's Premium Voyager. But space, service, and amenities vary. Also, some airlines may not offer a full first class experience but a hybrid of business and first, so it's advisable to check which features you'll receive for the extra money when booking.

You can secure good savings on internal or short-haul flights, when luxury, comfort and quality are lesser considerations, by traveling with a local low-cost airline.

> *Luxury travel is defined by experiences and destinations that take me completely away from my everyday life. It's not about expense or ostentation, but enjoying the very best of a location. It could be an astonishing meal in a San Sebastián restaurant, a beautifully designed room in a Caribbean hotel angled to attract the cooling sea breeze and bring the scent of evening blossoms, or even the services of a great river guide who can show the best fishing spots on private stretches of water. Luxury travel should mean you leave a destination knowing you have fully embraced its experiences, with memories that will last a lifetime.*

George Sell, editor BoutiqueHotelNews.com

Finding the Best Luxury Deals

Liberating luxury – finding luxury deals for less – is rewarding, exciting, and can be fun, especially when you think about how much you have saved compared to the person lying on the neighboring sun lounger. We know you'll be quietly smiling to yourself!

It doesn't have to be hard work. In fact, there are ways to take the effort out of it, such as finding agents to do the searching for you. But we've often found that the best deals are available through taking advantage of Do-It-Yourself packaging and flash sales. With a little know-how and time you can create a great vacation package for yourself.

Time is a key ingredient. The more time you have before your vacation, the better chance you have of tracking down fantastic deals. You may even discover a little gem of a hotel, villa, yacht charter or tour company that makes your trip all the more special.

How you decide to plan your vacation is up to you. It will largely depend on the time you have, what you want to do, where you want to go, and how confident you feel. Here are some tools for creating your trip, plus tips for maximizing the value that each has to offer.

Meet the Agent

For years agents were gatekeepers of travel goodness: the only people in the world whose tip-taps on computer keyboards could send you thousands of miles around the world to a tropical shore. But the internet almost consigned travel agents to history.

There are still plenty of travel agents and independent travel consultants around who do a fantastic job. They are travel professionals with access to up-to-the-minute information on your resort, hotel, and airline. Professionals who know a region or type of vacation – say, the wine regions of France, or religious or cultural tours to Israel - are worth their weight in gold, particularly as they likely have strong contacts on the ground to secure great prices and ensure your trip runs smoothly.

The experience, connections, and security of booking through an agent are clear. However, in our experience, agents have been undermined by technology as well as changes in the way they are paid by travel companies, and rarely offer the best value for money. While agents can come up with some good package deals with flights and transfers included, and still book the lion's share of cruise vacations (85 percent[26]), there are problems with their business model for consumers.

Part of what travel agents do is negotiate bulk purchases on beds at hotels and seats on planes and then package them for the forthcoming season. You'd imagine that this discounted rate would be passed on to the consumer, but this is not necessarily so.

Companies and individual agents need to make money too. After adding a percentage to the hotel rate and paying the consultants their commission –

usually around 10-18 percent – the price you pay can be quite high. And, given that many airlines have stopped paying commissions to agents, you may also have a percentage or flat-rate fee added to your airfare price.

The majority of online travel booking sites, such as Expedia and Travelocity, are, in fact, travel agencies, just without the overhead of operating premises on every high street and employing thousands of staff. This is part of the reason why online rates are so competitive.

> ### Liberate Luxury:
> If what you want is very specialized or you don't have time to research deals, an agent is probably a good idea. However, if you have the time to research carefully, you will likely get more luxury for less money by planning your trip yourself.

Package Your Own Vacation

We're big fans of what's become known as DIY-packaging: searching for your flight, hotel, car rental, transfers, and airport parking online and booking it yourself either with online agencies or directly with the provider.

We've been DIY-packaging our trips for about a decade, saving thousands of dollars each and every year.

DIY packages can be involved or straightforward – a month-long tour of South Africa will take time to research and find the best deal. A weekend in New York is a much easier proposition. So why not start with small trips? Then, as you build your skills, take on more complex arrangements where you have to match flight times to check-in days, rental car pick-ups, and more.

By packaging your own luxury trip you get to choose the vacation you want. Unrestricted by travel companies' pre-packaged deals, you get your choice of airport, airline and accommodation, on the day you want, for as long as suits you.

DIY-packaging does take tenacity and requires more than looking at the websites of one or two of the larger online agents to find the best value. It requires a strategy.

Our 12-Point Plan to Packaging Your Vacation and Finding the Best Deals Online

1. Be flexible. You may not always know where you want to go, but you may have a wish list. On other occasions, you know where you want to go, but can be flexible on dates. The more flexible you are regarding destination, dates, type of accommodation, and location, the easier it will be for you to find a luxury deal. Feel free to search for hotels to get an idea of the total cost of your trip, but always book flights first. It is easy to cancel a hotel or change bookings, but it's difficult and often costly to change flights.

2. Start your search by checking the larger travel agent websites (e.g., Expedia, Travelocity, Ebookers, Orbitz and Opodo) to get an idea of current pricing, any hot deals, or exceptional hotels they have on offer. We've often found great deals with both Expedia and Ebookers. When searching for a flight start with comparison sites like Skyscanner, Cheapflights, Hipmunk, Kayak and TravelSupermarket. You can also sign up for e-mail alerts about price changes on your chosen route.

3. Compare the cost of online travel agent packages to the cost of getting flights and hotels separately. Online agents can package some gems, such as our two-week trip to Antalya, Turkey, which cost $1,085 for flights and bed and breakfast in a five-star Sheraton hotel.

4. Don't search for the same flights or accommodation on the same dates too often from the same computer. Websites deposit cookies onto your computer and this can trigger increased fares if there's a lot of interest in flights or accommodation from your computer on a given day.

5. Be sure you know exactly where your flight is landing in relation to where you plan to stay. Be particularly aware of this if using low-cost airlines as they can land in different towns to what you might expect. Milan Bergamo, anyone? Use Google Earth or Google Maps to check the location of your hotel. Is it near a city centre, perfectly remote, or on the beach? How long will it take to get there from the airport?

6. Cover all options and check prices on airline and accommodation websites. In our experience it is exceptional to find the best deals this way. However, the travel industry is constantly changing, with US airlines in particular highlighting low fares on their own websites.

7. Book your flights once you've found them at an acceptable price. Hotels are easy to find, even if it's just days until your trip. Be mindful of large events or conferences happening in the area during your stay though, as accommodation will become booked up and expensive. If you know there's an event in town, check hotel availability before booking flights.

8. Check lots of websites when searching for a hotel. We usually check Booking, LateRooms, Room77, Octopus, Hotels, Lastminute, Trivago, Agoda, Venere and Travel Republic. We could go on – it seems there are new hotel booking sites launching every month. Some may be better in one destination than others, but keep in mind that just because you lucked out on a site with your last booking, it doesn't mean that you will again, so shop around. If you're not happy with the prices you're finding, a web search for something like "Paris hotels" will reveal sites you've never heard of – specialists in a particular region who have often negotiated spectacular rates. Alternatively, think outside the box and search online for serviced apartments or home rentals.

9. Narrow your hotel search by checking reviews on the booking site and traveler review sites such as TripAdvisor. Sadly, reviews on the site have not always been the most reliable. But sites like TripAdvisor are one of the few places you can get a feel for a hotel; just try to take a measure of the reviews and look to the middle ground, be it largely positive or negative. Also, check other online sources such as newspapers, magazines, blogs, and guides for information on your accommodation; a web search of its name should yield plenty of results.

10. Turn your attention to travel extras once flights and hotels are booked. Plan your route to the airport and book your parking or train tickets, allowing yourself plenty of time, perhaps enough to relax in an airport lounge or do a little tax-free shopping. Once you land, picking up a taxi at the airport is usually a straightforward, cost-effective option, but some accommodation can be a long distance from the nearest airport. In this

case, consider booking transfers in advance. We've listed companies in the Resources section that offer private and group transfers.

11. A value for money deal isn't a deal until all aspects have been factored in, so check prices from different airports. Perhaps flights into Newark, New Jersey, are significantly cheaper than into JFK in New York, making any extra expense and time involved in traveling into the city negligible. Consider the total trip price, including accommodation, flights, any hotels needed during layovers, car rentals, transfers via taxi or public transport, and airport parking. For example, we know parking at London Heathrow is significantly more expensive than parking at other London airports, so this could influence which airport we choose to depart from.

12. Don't forget to keep a record of all your flights, hotels, car rentals, etc. Place all the details in a spreadsheet, or use an app like Evernote or TripIt Pro, or good old fashioned pen and paper.

This plan has consistently worked for us and we hope you derive as much success from it as we have. Just don't tell people you meet on vacation how much you paid for your trip!

Using our 12-Point Plan we saved $4,650 on our southern African vacation. We were able to book a helicopter flight over Victoria Falls, in Zambia, and other luxury travel extras with the savings.

How to Save $4,650 in 11 Days

"Yes, let's go!" After weeks of deliberation we'd finally decided: we were going to South Africa for a month. As our plan developed, more destinations were added to our itinerary. We wanted to see Johannesburg, Cape Town, and Durban. We wanted to stay at the beach and go on a safari. It would be a complex trip and we expected it to cost a lot of money.

We gave our main street travel agent our wish list.

The agent gave us a great idea – to extend our trip with a couple of days at Victoria Falls in Zambia. But his total package would have cost $9,000, without rental cars and booking nearly a year in advance. And we were spending over a week of the trip staying with friends. We like luxury, but we didn't want to have to pay that much for it.

> ❝ *By packaging our vacation ourselves rather than buying from a travel agent we saved $4,650 - the equivalent of another trip.* ❞

Heading home, we set to work. By searching websites – booking with large online agencies and individual suppliers (such as a South African car rental firm) and using the country's excellent low-cost airline, Kulula, instead of forking out for unnecessary scheduled flights for short internal journeys - we found what the travel agent was offering and more.

We booked stays in excellent four- and five-star hotels, a beautifully secluded safari lodge, and a timeshare apartment in Durban that was large enough for our friends to share with us, and it cost less than half the price quoted by the travel agent - $4,350, to be precise.

Not only did we have plenty of money in the bank to splash out on a helicopter ride over Victoria Falls and more vacation treats, but we also felt good that we had succeeded in saving thousands of dollars.

Putting together our own package took work but it meant that we got exactly what we wanted at vastly reduced rates. Instead of paying $9,000, we paid $4,350. By packaging it ourselves rather than buying from a travel agent we saved $4,650 - the equivalent of another trip.

It's not often that you get the chance to save almost $5,000 in 11 days and have a fantastic vacation.

And the Savings Continued…

Since South Africa and Zambia we've organized trips all over the world, unearthing important tips along the way. On a vacation to New York and New Orleans we shifted our departure date to the very end of October to take advantage of low season fares, saving hundreds of dollars by simply leaving two weeks later.

When the strength of the Euro made visiting certain European countries expensive, we took advantage of cheaper destinations, visiting Turkey instead of Greece or Cyprus.

We've arranged everything from a long weekend in Paris to complicated multi-stop trips: to Greece, visiting Athens, flying to Santorini, booking a local hydrofoil service to Mykonos, then flying back home via Athens, and to Thailand, spending a few days in Bangkok, taking internal flights to Chiang Mai, then to Krabi, Koh Phi Phi, and back home via Bangkok three weeks later.

It hasn't all been plain sailing. We were terribly disappointed with the quality of our hotel in Santorini, so we immediately headed to the nearby town where we found a charming family-run hotel right on the beach. The owner even drove us back to the original hotel to help us collect our cases.

We also planned a seven-day trip to Barcelona and only booked six, and on another trip reserved a day's airport parking less than we needed. But things happen and these are pretty minor considering we've taken forty or more DIY trips.

View of the Bey Mountains from our junior suite at the five-star Sheraton Voyager, in Antalya, Turkey, where we stayed for two weeks for $1,085, including our flights.

Great Prices Gone in a Flash

Flash sales may have started as a way for airlines to offload unsold seats, but they have quickly become established in the wider travel market, with a host of companies now offering vastly reduced rates on accommodation for short periods of time.

Over the past five years the flash sale has become the hot travel booking trend. The Portrait of American Travelers 2010 report found that one in seven active travelers purchased a leisure travel service as a result of receiving a flash sale e-mail.[27] And with plush, inviting websites, luxurious accommodation and, most importantly, incredible discounts, it's easy to see why.

"After hotels reach a certain occupancy rate of say, 70 percent, they are happy to offer flash sales to fill remaining occupancy," says Tom Valentine, managing director of luxury travel club Secret Escapes. "This means we're able to supply luxury at standard three-star prices."

The benefits of flash sales, aside from the price cuts, are that these companies excel at sourcing the newest, most exciting destinations and chic hotels. They also encourage you to try somewhere new, or a destination you might otherwise have overlooked.

"I don't think value is king," explained Valentine, summing up the flash sale phenomenon. "But few people have enough money not to have to source a good deal. Sometimes people are just looking for a different experience and this is the value of flash sales."

Groupon may be the best known flash sale company with daily deals on everything from mattresses to Zumba classes. The company partnered with Expedia to launch Groupon Getaways, offering quality vacations as part of Groupon's "buy today, gone tomorrow" model. Competitors offer a similar service, such as LivingSocial's LivingSocial Escapes, though many of their deals are for US cities only.

Travelzoo is perhaps one of the earliest-known flash sale sites, wowing over 25 million subscribers with weekly deals. But with a crop of sites launching, it's become a very competitive market with lots of choice – which is good news for travelers.

The best way to plan a vacation using flash sales is to sign up to as many companies as your inbox can handle; they each send weekly e-mails as a minimum.

You never know when one of them will have a hotel in a destination that appeals to you, with a 75 percent reduction. Plus, flash sellers like to lure you in with little extras so look out for things like free champagne on arrival, a complimentary dinner for two or free spa treatments.

Flash sales are always a good deal, but be aware that they don't always amount to the percentage discount shown. According to a study of 100 deals from Groupon, Travelzoo, and LivingSocial by travel market researchers PhoCusWright, the deals were generally good but discounts were not as favorable as advertised in about 10 percent of cases. They are often based on hotel rack rates or brochure prices for packages.[28]

We think that a good deal is a good deal regardless. Just do your research to see if you can secure an even bigger discount, and always read the fine print before purchasing as flash sales can have restrictions such as dates of travel.

Our Favorite Flash Sale Websites

Secret Escapes releases some daily deals but most go live on Mondays and run for a week. They hand pick four- and five-star or luxury boutique hotel deals around the world and also offer flight inclusive packages. The website negotiates great value extras such as room upgrades, complimentary massages, excursions, meals, and rooms with views. Members can 'hold' a booking for $39 until they book, when the fee is deducted from their purchase.

Jetsetter claims up to 50 percent off the most luxurious hotels around the world with sales lasting from five to seven days. The company's vacations range from tracking the big five in Kenya, to family city tours in Italy, to treks to Everest Base Camp in Nepal with luxury specialists Abercrombie & Kent, to breaks to one of our hot destinations, Greece's Costa Navarino.

TripAlertz is part flash sales, part group-buying (the more people buy a deal the cheaper it becomes). Its most talked of deal was a once-in-a-lifetime trip to space for $95,000.

Voyage Privé claims up to 75 percent off upscale breaks, each vetted by their team of travel agents. It has attracted more than six million members to the free-to-join travel club.

Vacationist proclaims savings of up to 60 percent on their luxury accommodation and has the backing of Travel + Leisure magazine.

Other sites you may wish to consider are listed in the Resources section of this book and at livesharetravel.com/luxury-travel.

Benefit from Your Loyalty

Do Hilton hotels make you happy? Are you a fan of Fairmont? Do you think W stands for wonderful? If you like to book with a particular brand when you travel, why not benefit from your loyalty?

Loyalty programs from airlines, hotels, credit cards and even supermarkets can provide great travel savings for little effort.

Working on the simple premise that every flight or hotel stay with a company earns miles or points which can be redeemed against future travels, loyalty programs can save you thousands of dollars on your vacations or allow you to upgrade for a more luxurious trip.

Another benefit of belonging to a loyalty program is that you will receive regular offers from the travel company and can often access special privileges such as upgraded seats on flights or priority boarding, or gain complimentary business or executive floor benefits, such as free Wi-Fi or pre-dinner cocktails.

You may not have the time and tenacity of a travel hacker – people constantly chasing miles or points and elite status to game the system – but you can still make loyalty programs work for you.

Our 12-Point Plan to Loyalty Programs

Depending on the plan, loyalty programs offer the opportunity to earn points or miles when you make a purchase. Though most allow you to use points or miles as total payment for travel or other rewards, some also allow you to use a combination of points/miles plus cash. Want to use your loyalty to liberate luxury? Follow our plan.

1. Choose an airline or hotel brand you're happy to travel with regardless of the loyalty program. Using them regularly will help you collect points/miles quickly.

2. Most airlines are members of an airline alliance (Star Alliance, oneworld or SkyTeam). Join one program per alliance and you can earn and redeem with each airline in that alliance. Try to keep most of your points with your preferred airline as you can use them for other benefits, such as priority boarding. With hotels, you'll find that many brands are owned by one company (e.g., Starwood includes Westin, Sheraton and W Hotels). Keep it in the family by staying with other brands in the group.

3. When flying with an airline or staying at a hotel whose loyalty program you don't belong to, collect the points/miles anyway. Loyalty programs are free to join and you just never know when they might prove useful.

4. Bear in mind that loyalty flights and upgrades could cost less with one of your favorite airlines' sister companies.

5. Be aware that hotel programs run on a varied basis ranging from points per spend to a flat number of points per night of stay. And some only give you points when you book directly with them.

6. Upgrade your membership – go for gold, platinum or elite status – to the highest level possible. This will increase the types of rewards

available to you, from priority check-in, to priority boarding and better seats, to late check-out and all those executive floor benefits. Collecting the necessary points/miles may seem tricky at first but following Tip #2 will help.

7. Share a single hotel account with family members, so if you take trips separately you can maximize the points earned.

8. Sign up for e-mail alerts from your loyalty program for updates on point sales and bonus opportunities.

9. Get a credit card that gives you points with your favorite airline or hotel. This doesn't have to be the travel company's own card; many credit cards offer schemes with travel discounts.

10. When redeeming points, always check the difference between coach and business or first class. We recently discovered the price of a one-way coach flight from New York to London was worth 70,000 points, but a business class ticket (the best in-flight cabin available on this airline/route) was only 10,000 points more. That's a lot of luxury for not many more points.

11. Choose a hotel program that offers benefits you particularly value. Late check-out is great but aren't free stays or miles you can transfer to your airline program more valuable?

12. If you only spend on hotels or flights once or twice a year the chances of building up to a great reward in a hurry are slim. It might be better to opt for a program that offers other awards such as merchandise or gift cards.

Our Favorite Loyalty Programs

Virgin Atlantic's points have a long shelf life; in fact, they never expire as long as you fly with the airline or one of its partners every three years. Virgin has many partners with whom you can earn points, offering everything from groceries to financial products, and run pretty reasonable cash plus points and points only sales.

United Airlines have low taxes and fees on loyalty redemption, and plenty of flexibility including the use of one-way rewards, roundtrip tickets including layovers, and open tickets.[29]

Hilton HHonors is the only program that counts award stays towards elite status so you can work your way to the top even on a free stay. Stay credits can also be used with more than 60 airlines.

Starwood's Cash & Points program lets you book a stay with as few as 2,000 points, and allows you to top up with cash when you're short on points. Added to that, there are no blackout days so you can book an award stay whenever you wish.

Hyatt also allows you to travel anytime with no blackout dates and gives their Elite Diamond members four upgrades a year on paid suites. Their program allows you to convert points into miles with thirty airlines.

Feel the Fear and Do It Anyway...

Liberating luxury travel – finding ways to see the world for less and in style – is a recipe with three ingredients. It requires one part know-how, one part tenacity and a good sprinkle of confidence. But it's very rewarding, especially when you consider taking your next great vacation without spending a fortune - not to mention the thrill of seeing new places and spending fun times with family and friends.

Here we explore the third element of the liberating luxury mix: confidence. The more you travel, the more you realize people are largely the same the world over. Yes, differences in language, religion, wealth, and culture exist. But we all feel the same attachments to family, friends and society.

On your travels you will largely find people who are friendly, welcoming and helpful. Yes, just like at home, you'll find scammers, pickpockets and unsavory sorts. But you'll mostly find people delighted that you're visiting their country and willing to do what they can to help you enjoy your stay.

Hotel Hell

If you have issues with your room, a health problem, trouble with your luggage, need to reconfirm your flights or anything else, the hotel staff should be well-equipped to assist.

Some people fear that their airline, hotel or other accommodation might not be up to scratch when booking online. In all of our years of travel, we have naturally experienced this situation. But only once!

There are no guarantees that a package would serve you better in this regard. Travel companies have been known to send people to half-built hotels. When booking your hotel, do your research via online reviews and blogs and you should have a great experience. You can even use Google Street View to see street-level images of your hotel and the surroundings.

Secure Buying Online

Trojans, worms, viruses, identity theft and more have heightened people's fear of shopping online. Some also worry that they might not get what they pay for. We've thankfully never had any such problems, but will deal with consumer safety and protection in depth in section 4, "Playing it Safe".

Before booking, ensure that a web page is secure. It should have "https" at the start of the URL (website address) or the padlock symbol should be visible in your browser. Don't make a payment on a site that does not have one or the other of these.

We strongly recommend using a credit card for the majority of bookings online. The only time we consider not using one is when a travel company puts hefty administration fees on credit card transactions, at which point we see if they offer any free methods of payment such as PayPal. But paying by credit card is ideal.

Credit cards offer more protection from services not rendered than most other forms of payment. For example, a sudden closure of an airline can leave refund-seekers waiting behind a long list of creditors, and there's no guarantee of a refund. Laws differ in every country but in the US, for example, credit card users typically have sixty days from the date the charge is posted to their account to dispute it against a service not rendered under the Fair Credit Billing Act.[30] Some credit cards also offer additional travel protection. Check with your card issuer about such services.

Negotiating Arrivals

One of the biggest issues people have when planning a non-packaged vacation is their arrival. Here, package vacation offer something of a security blanket. You walk off the plane, amble through arrivals and find smiling travel representatives waiting for you. They take you on buses to your hotel and help you check in. Then, certainly by the end of your first day, there's the welcome meeting where they tell you about the hotel, resort area, region, local customs and available activities and trips.

Ask yourself how important this is to you. Could you manage on your own, even in a land where you don't speak the language?

Sure you could.

Let's take transfers first. There are perhaps a handful of tiny, insignificant airports in the world which do not have a long line of taxis waiting outside and excellent public transport links. Taxi drivers know the area inside out, are delighted to have a fare and will whisk you to your hotel in comfort - and in half the time of a transfer bus, which will leave you sitting, often in steamy conditions, while you await the rest of your group.

Always use official taxis as signposted in the airport. Unofficial taxis may try to rip you off. Make sure you know roughly where your hotel is, at least which area of town it's in. You'll find the name of your hotel, the address, and sometimes a map on the voucher you print after making your booking. Show it to the driver to avoid confusion.

If you're really traveling in style the hotel may provide a private transfer by luxury car, or you can arrange one yourself with a local company. This will also reduce the amount of time you spend in the airport before your return flight, leaving you more time by the pool; those taking package vacations often have to leave hours ahead of their flight to pick up other travelers en route.

As for the welcome meeting hosted by travel representatives, many travelers realize that one of the main aims of the meeting is to sell you tours. We've rarely attended a welcome meeting that provided information on the hotel, resort or region that we had not, or could not have discovered from another source. This is largely what your hotel concierge is for.

So what are you waiting for? The world is out there for you to explore. Get online and book your luxury vacation today.

Having the confidence to book your own travels can lead to enchanting, authentic experiences. We met this farming couple high in Austria's Tirol mountains, drank milk fresh from their cows and sampled their homemade bread and cheese.

Liberate Luxury with these Additional Tips

- Consider destinations where your national currency is strong against the local currency.

- Certain days of the week are recommended as the best for booking flights or accommodation, others as the best days to travel. Sundays are said to be favorable for cheap hotel rates. Tuesdays and Wednesdays are said to be the best for booking a flight, and there is anecdotal evidence that they are the most economical days to fly.

- If dealing with an agent, hotelier or villa owner directly, always ask for a discount. If you don't ask, they won't offer.

- When arranging packages yourself, either by DIY-packaging or putting together elements of flash sales or loyalty programs, allow yourself enough travel time – an absolute minimum of two hours before a flight, between connecting flights, etc. When taking a cruise it's best to arrive the day before departure, particularly if you're traveling long-haul.

- Thoroughly check your dates, arrival times, departure and arrival cities for each leg of your journey. A friend once saw an amazing flight to Athens. After she booked it, she realized that it was to Athens, Georgia in the US, not Athens, Greece. Also, double-check the small print before paying for your trip. Make sure you understand exactly what you're buying.

- **Always purchase travel insurance** – it is perhaps the most important thing you'll book for your vacation. Medical fees abroad can be heart-stoppingly high so make sure your policy has plenty of medical cover. Insurance is usually better value when purchased from a third party than through your airline or travel company.

> *Luxury means offering something few others can, catering to my every need, often before I even know what that need is. A luxury travel experience means not having to worry about anything, not having to do anything I don't want to, anticipating my needs and then exceeding them. Whatever your definition of luxury is, it's aspirational. Whether that be an extra half meter on your caravan, or a penthouse at The Ritz, people will always try to experience that little bit extra. Perhaps in the prevailing economic climate people have had to redefine what luxury is to them, but the desire to experience something luxurious will always be there.*

Matt Holmes of luxury exchange program, The Registry Collection

Sarah & Terry Lee

LIVING LUXURY

"We live in an age when unnecessary things are our only necessities."

Oscar Wilde,
The Picture of Dorian Gray

Black and white murals at Hotel Convento La Magdalena, in Antequera, Spain.

Seven Hot Trends in Luxury Travel

The luxury travel industry is constantly transforming to meet customers' evolving demands. "From observing both the high-end private residence club and boutique hotel markets over the last couple of years, it's clear luxury travel has become a much more 'experiential' commodity," says George Sell, editor of BoutiqueHotelNews.com.

"Those with the financial means to travel to high-end destinations are less interested in ostentatious display, but more in amassing memories which will stay with them. Hotels and private residence clubs are offering more activities and trips to guests – from heli-skiing to pampering spa offers."

According to *The Future of Luxury Travel*, a report by the International Luxury Travel Market,[31] you can expect to find the following trends in the luxury sector:

- **Personal service.** While the style of service may vary, there's an increasing global demand for more customized, highly-personalized services.

- **Out with ostentation.** More privacy and a quieter, more discreet style of luxury are preferred by travelers. There is a growing demand among younger travelers for simple and transparent products and services. This combines with the development of ethical and environmental values and the increasing demand for authentic and personal experiences.

- **Simplicity and seamless service rank highly.** With time the most precious commodity, travel providers are working hard to ensure all elements of the luxury service work seamlessly together.

- **The big country.** There's an increase in interest in open-range excursions. Destinations such as Brazil, Argentina/Chile (Patagonia), Australia and New Zealand are growing in popularity for their spectacular landscapes and unspoiled natural attractions.

- **Less ordinary.** There's a growing interest in off-the-beaten-track destinations, appealing to environmentally-concerned and culturally-interested travelers. These include destinations with fascinating cultures and traditions, such as Israel and Peru, and those actively working to protect nature and endangered animal species.

- **Extended planning.** The luxury travel industry anticipates growth in the coming years, sparking a gradual rise in advance booking times and rates.

- **Cyber travel.** An awareness of value will continue to impact travel decisions, and the internet and social media will remain major influences on planning and booking.

Get Packing

You've planned your trip, it's the night before you fly, and you're buzzing with pre-vacation excitement. But whatever will you wear? A luxury vacation may seem the perfect occasion to wear designer finery and jewels that will dazzle as much as the tropical sunshine. After all, you'll be staying in unrivaled accommodation, so certain attire may be expected, and you want to look your best. But over-dressing may not be wise or appropriate and, as we discuss in the next section, "Playing it Safe", it could invite unwanted attention.

It is always advisable to research cultural and religious requirements of the local dress code when visiting, for instance, Muslim countries and/or religious sites anywhere in the world. You'll often find a relaxation of such rules within the confines of hotels; just be aware and respectful of local customs.

In the vast majority of luxury accommodations the dress code is largely casual. Yes, you'll often be expected to dress for dinner, perhaps wear trousers rather than shorts, and swimwear is frowned upon in restaurants, no matter what time of day. But most hotels and certainly villas, glampsites and yachts would expect little more than smart casual clothing.

Hotels: There are, of course, exceptions to every rule. At some five-star hotels, such as The Ritz in London, jeans and sports shoes are not permitted and gentlemen are required to wear a tie in certain lounges and restaurants. Some hotels in hot countries, such as the four-star Mango Bay in Barbados, and Lebua at State Tower in Bangkok, ban open-toed shoes.

Luxury Trains: These are often relaxed, but the sophisticated Orient-Express requires a little more wardrobe consideration. "Think work wear for the day and black tie for the evening," says Jools Stone of TrainsontheBrain.com. "Men have it easy – you can't go wrong with a tuxedo, the main question is white or black. I went for black for sheer convenience but there's a lot to be said for the full-on white James Bond number. Some chaps even wore fairly ordinary looking work suits. But for women the sky's the limit, and as the Orient-Express states – it's impossible to overdress for the Orient-Express."[32]

Cruise Ships: Usually require a similar sense of style and are traditionally the place you'd find travelers not just dressing for dinner, but making it a tastefully-styled event with dinner suits, tuxedos (though white jackets are traditionally reserved for summer nights), and cocktail dresses de rigueur.

Few cruise ships are quite as prescriptive as Cunard, which states that on a typical seven-night cruise you can expect three formal, two semi-formal, and two elegant casual evenings. Formal is essentially black tie for men and evening dress for ladies, while military or award decorations may also be worn. Semi-formal calls for jackets and ties for gentlemen and cocktail dresses or trouser suits for ladies, but strictly no jeans. Elegant casual means jackets with no tie for men, and dresses, skirts or trousers for ladies, but again, no jeans.[33]

Other cruise lines, however, take a more relaxed approach. On Princess, Carnival, and Royal Caribbean, a lounge suit is perfectly acceptable for dressy evenings, while Norwegian Cruise Line's Freestyle Cruises have pioneered a dress up or go casual policy. Look out for dress code information in your cruise ship's daily newspaper, or on your in-room television system.

It's About the Journey

T.S. Eliot is credited with saying: "the journey, not the arrival, matters," espousing the virtues of the act of traveling. Luckily for him he didn't have to put up with the complexities and frustrations of getting from A to B in the 21st century.

There is little that is luxurious about the airport experience. You may face long check-in lines, officious security staff, invasive security screening, overpriced restaurants, busy departure lounges, and planes full of screaming babies. But there are little ways in which you can ease your path.

Start Your Journey Right

Many luxury travel companies now offer chauffeured transfers from your home to the airport, allowing you to relax from the get-go.

If you prefer to drive, meet and greet parking is a fantastic way to reduce stress levels on arrival at the airport. Instead of dropping your car at a parking lot up to twenty minutes away from the terminal and waiting for a transfer, a driver will meet you seconds from the check-in desks, then return your car to you when you arrive back at the airport. We've tried both chauffeurs and meet and greet services at a number of airports and are big fans of these options.

Glide Through Security

Security has become one of the most hideous, albeit necessary, evils of travel. We all appreciate the need for tightened measures and that security staff have an important job to do, but each time we travel, security seems to get worse. There is little standardization of checks, so you never know exactly what to expect and can't be prepared. Only some airports require the removal of shoes and belts, for example, while surly staff yell at you for the merest mistake.

Thanks to fast-tracking there is another way. The security checks are no less thorough; but the reduction in the number of people through that channel relieves the stress and time it takes. Fast-tracked security is routinely available "by invitation only" – read for first and business class passengers – or holders of medium to elite airline loyalty program status. However, some airports offer access to the fast-track lane for a small fee. In our minds, it's worth every penny.

Hit the Lounge

If you're flying first or business class, you can leave the hustle and bustle of departures behind for the seclusion and comfort of an airport lounge.

Services vary greatly, from the airport's own serviced lounges, to the full-scale glamor of airline-run ones like Virgin's super-chic Clubhouse at major international airports. Lounges can have it all, from hot showers to relaxation areas, the business pages to free Wi-Fi, massages to private transfers by Mercedes to your plane, alongside an excellent selection of food and well-stocked bars.

Again, even though you might not be flying first or business class, you can take advantage of airport lounge services by either booking in advance online, paying a fee at the airport or using a card like Priority Pass, which has various annual memberships allowing access to lounges around the world.

Knowing When to Spend – Shopping and Currency

You may love shopping at the airport, and though tax-free shopping isn't always what it's cracked up to be, there can be some good buys.

Something that never offers good value at an airport, however, is currency exchange. Rates at an airport currency exchange counter are inexplicably poorer than what you receive via an ATM at the airport or at a bank in town. Today it's just as easy, and largely cost-effective, to travel with your bank debit card as to use outdated traveler's checks.

Money cards are a recent addition to vacation finance. These cards work just like debit cards except that you stock them with cash online before or during your journey. You can then withdraw money in the local currency at ATMs or use them to pay for goods, meals and services. The cards usually also work as MasterCard or Visa debit cards, which are widely accepted just about anywhere - but do check in advance that they will work in the destination you're planning to travel to. Depending on the card, you'll pay a small annual fee or commission on withdrawals, but they offer a healthy exchange rate and are a safe way to carry your money.

Parking to Check-In

Accustomed as we were to off-site airport parking and being bused to the terminal – adding up to an hour each way to our journey – we were delighted to discover meet and greet airport parking.

Meteor Meet and Greet was more expensive than off-site parking, but having saved on our trip to Dubai we thought we'd try it.

> ❝ *We set off on our walk to the terminal. It took about 30 seconds.* ❞

It was an early departure, and as we fought our way through London's rush hour traffic, Sarah called to tell our Meteor guy that we were ten minutes from the airport. "Pull up in the drop-off area outside the terminal and I'll meet you there," he said.

We drove past signs for long-stay parking, beyond the medium-stay parking lots. We even bypassed the short-stay options, stopping right outside the airport. There was a part of me that couldn't believe we were in the right place. I quizzed Sarah: "Did he really say he'd meet us here?"

Sure enough, our guy was there, meeting and greeting us outside the terminal. After inspecting the car he gave me a receipt in exchange for my keys and reminded us to call when we returned.

We set off on our walk to the terminal. It took about 30 seconds. A travel luxury if ever there was one! From parking to joining the line for check-in took a total of four minutes. We could barely believe how easy it was.

And it was just as simple on our return: we were met right where we'd parked the car, the driver only handing over the keys when we showed our receipt.
We loved the luxury of convenience, saving time, not worrying whether a parking lot bus would get us to the terminal in good time, and the fact that within a few minutes of landing we were on the road heading home.

How to Get an Upgrade

The eternal travel quandary! Everyone wants to know how to get a complimentary upgrade to their flight, hotel or cruise accommodation.

It's a question we're asked frequently and we could probably charge good money for the magic formula. It's a tip we'd happily share, but unfortunately we can't because we've never been given a free upgrade. Not on a flight at least.

It's not that we haven't tried. We've smiled sweetly at check-in, dressed smartly, even cheekily asked if there are spare seats in first class. But the only upgrade we've ever had on a flight is one that we've paid for.

Sean Tipton of the Association of British Travel Agents has this advice: "Always be polite. 'Do you know who I am?' never works. Often airlines will aim their upgrades at business travelers, so dressing smartly helps. Also, from my own personal experience, being visibly upset and crying helps – it got a friend of mine into first class on a flight back to New Zealand."

We're not completely convinced that there is a magic formula, rather a combination of good fortune and airline economics. Routes to first class upgrades we've heard of include:

1. Arriving at the airport early. Any available upgraded seats are distributed early on.

2. Being a member of the airline's loyalty program.

3. Being lucky – for example, traveling on a flight that's oversold in economy but has seats remaining in business or first class.

4. Traveling alone, or rather, without children. Kids are an upgrade barrier.

5. Looking the part. Being smartly attired in business wear can get you places. Airlines are more willing to upgrade passengers who look as though they will fit in.

6. Generally being polite and helpful to other passengers and airline staff.

7. Being badly inconvenienced on your previous flight, for example, if your flight with the same or a sister airline was late. Just don't make a fuss, or else it could work against you.

We're pleased to say that we've had much more success in gaining upgrades on our accommodation – from standard rooms to suites, and from no view to sparkling sea view. Make hotels and cruise companies aware of special occasions you may be celebrating while with them. Even if you don't get a full upgrade, you will likely be greeted with at least a bottle of wine or champagne in your room. But upgrades from a standard room to a suite are likely; they want you to have happy memories of your important day so you return in years to come.

A small upgrade point of note: whenever you book a rental car, always take the minimum car type that you can cope with. We've had our cars upgraded free of charge on nearly every booking we've made.

Swimming pool at The Chedi, Muscat in Oman.

A Stylish Stay – Hotels and Cruises

When traveling in luxury, accommodation should always amount to more than just a place to lay your head. Even downright serviceable four-star hotels should be spotlessly clean and offer a few extra amenities or services for the price tag.

Get a Room

Room sizes vary around the world, and often the smaller rooms found in the old buildings of cheek-by-jowl European cities leave US visitors – accustomed to plenty of space in even the most standard hotel room – dismayed.

Hotels have a number of different room types, some offering more floor space, others with upgraded features and facilities - and then there are suites and penthouses. Rooms can also be categorized by bed type, such as king, queen, double and single. However, the same type of room can amount to different standards in different hotels. Here's the break-down:

Standard rooms or those described as 'run of house' are usually the most basic room type offered and have rudimentary amenities and furnishings. Naturally, a standard room at an upscale brand would generally be of a higher quality than a less exclusive one, but standard rooms in better quality hotels usually won't come with a view.

Superior rooms should be an upgrade on a standard room in both size and furnishings, but it often refers to just the view.

Deluxe rooms should have striking views, be well-positioned – not next to a noisy lift, for example – and be spacious with upgraded furnishings. But be aware that some Caribbean hotels rank deluxe as a lower category than a superior room.

Junior suites are typically larger, with a seating area sometimes separated by a small dividing wall.

Studios are similar to junior suites, but come with the added advantage of cooking facilities.

Suites will usually have a minimum of two rooms, such as a bedroom and living room.

Penthouses are defined as the ultimate in hotel luxury with designer interiors, fixtures and fittings, and standout attractions such as rooftop pools, bowling lanes or any number of other fabulous features.

Executive, business, or club floors invariably target the business traveler with additions such as free Wi-Fi or a business suite with printing and other facilities, and are a quieter space away from families and groups. Executive floors can be great for luxury leisure travelers as well, with additions such as private check-in, butler service, greater in-room space, and a lounge serving anything from breakfast to afternoon tea to pre-dinner cocktails.

The penthouse suite aboard Celebrity Solstice. Features include a baby grand piano, double balcony with whirlpool bath, a television set in the bathroom wall, and butler service.

Rooms with a Sea View

Room types on cruise ships are broadly similar to hotels, with everything from single staterooms (on a handful of ships) to duplexes, penthouses and apartments with their own swimming pools or outdoor hot tubs. There are two key things to consider: space is at a premium on ships and standard staterooms are rarely large. If you like space, upgrade your room type. Also, be aware that not all staterooms have sea views or a balcony. All-balcony ships are becoming more prevalent, but if you want to truly take in the sea air, opt for at least an outside stateroom with a porthole.

The Star System

Luxury is defined in very different ways by every airline, cruise ship and hotel – sometimes even within the same brand. Where a four-star boutique hotel may only have double-bedded rooms with a shower and no view from a small window, another hotel wouldn't dream of providing anything less than a queen-size bed, designer fixtures and fittings, whirlpool bath and a view you'd pay money for, through panoramic floor to ceiling windows.

Star ratings were devised to help travelers decipher the difference between hotels and the services they offer. Though they currently provide the best and most internationally-utilized system, they're not a straightforward guide.

"There is no international star rating guide," explains Sean Tipton of the Association of British Travel Agents. "In most countries, the ratings are given by local tourist boards. So a five-star hotel in Kenya may not be as high a standard as one in Europe, but should be of a higher standard than lower-rated hotels in its own country. You will see an improving standard of décor, food and general service as you climb the rating scale."

Years ago this scale stopped at four-star; then, five-star promised the ultimate in excellence. In recent years this has been usurped by six- and seven-star ratings for hotels in Europe and the Middle East.

Some believe that such star-rating inflation is more for the benefit of hotels than their guests; part of the problem being that no one can agree on what the stars represent.

European countries such as Spain, France, Greece, Italy, Portugal, Malta, the Netherlands, Belgium, Denmark and Hungary have nationally standardized rating systems. In Britain, the system has been established by the Automobile Association (AA) and the national tourist boards, while the US has several organizations awarding stars.

Meanwhile, travel websites and agents often have their own systems based on their inspection visits and other data, adding greater confusion to the mix – particularly when a hotel has differing star ratings. Few explain their ratings system, and though it's refreshing to see Expedia's description of theirs, the disclaimer that goes with it – "Some criteria may vary from country to country. Our hotel star rating classifications are not a representation or promise of any particular feature or amenity,"[34] – is not especially helpful.

Yet a hotel's star rating is perhaps the first thing you look at when booking. We've done it ourselves – judged the inherent quality of one hotel over another based on its stars.

This is clearly something the global travel industry needs to standardize for it to prove a truly useful measure for travelers.

In the meantime, perhaps the key is to never judge a book by its five-star cover and, instead, to assess its facilities, photos and reviews before booking.

Five Luxury Mysteries, by Sarah

> **"** *Short of Elvis-styled emergencies, I can't see myself using the phone while on the throne.* **"**

I love luxury hotels: the sense of opulence as you sweep into the lobby, the cool design touches in your room, everything from the big facilities like split-level spas to the tiny extras like the odd but creative animal figures chambermaids make out of your towels each day.

But there are some features of five-star hotels around the world that I just can't fathom:

- The number and complexity of light switches. I once stayed in a room with 23 light switches. Why? That's more light switches than I have in my entire house. There really is no need, and I wasn't the only one to spend a long time trying to figure out the sequence to turn them off before bed on the first night of my stay. One switch by the bed that turns off every light in the room will do nicely – 23 is neither cool, nor clever.

- Double rooms with single beds. When you book a double room to share a bed with your loved one, why do you sometimes find there are two beds pushed closely together? Though you try to push them together completely, it never works if you have to battle with two sets of sheets, and the fear that one of you will inevitably fall through the gap in the dead of night.

- Poor quality gyms. I find it inexplicable that quality hotels with great facilities can often have shoddy gyms. Not only are they under-equipped but on more than one occasion I've spotted an exercise bike, changed into my gym gear and hopped on the bike to find the foot straps missing, and my feet sliding off the pedals.

- A nice cuppa. Forget making your own drinks. Tea and coffee making facilities are hard to find in-room, with some hotels only providing them in their suites. Come on, we're British – we need tea!

- Telephones in bathrooms. This is a sign of a true luxury hotel, and is very popular in Spain. But short of any Elvis-styled emergencies, I really can't see myself using the phone while on the throne. Never. Ever.

An Aladdin's lamp shaped tea-pot at the Sheraton Porto Hotel & Spa, in Portugal. But like other five-star hotels there were no tea-making facilities in-room, causing us to use up one of our three wishes straight away.

A Luxury Service

Part of what defines the luxury experience is that travel providers offer guests outstanding or unique services that they would not find elsewhere. Some of these things are all part of the service, others may come with a fee.

Mine the Concierge

In hotels the concierge should be your go-to person for any request. They provide in-depth knowledge of your destination and services beyond the limits of most reception desks, such as securing tickets for a theatre show or reservations at a popular restaurant. Hotel concierges are a mine of information, so use them. They're paid for their exceptional insider knowledge and contacts – from personal shoppers to restaurant maître d's – and for achieving the impossible.

Restaurants are more likely to accommodate last minute requests from a concierge they're used to doing business with than individuals they don't know. Concierges can really come into their own, however, when you call ahead of your stay and discuss your plans with them. They may be able to point you in the direction of discounts or savings at local attractions. This will also give them time to get you tickets to a sold-out show.

Usually part of a global network, under the umbrella of organizations like the Clefs d'Or, concierges regularly work with colleagues around the world to ensure that clients are well taken care of wherever they travel.

Technology Delivering Luxury

Luxury travel is increasingly dominated by the latest technology, be that in the way the industry delivers the luxury experience or in terms of amenities provided in-room.

Some hotels have iPhone apps through which you can request any hotel service. There are also in-room smart systems that automatically adjust the lighting, room temperature and music to the preference of frequent visitors, so that they feel completely at home upon checking in.

The Eccleston Square Hotel describes itself as London's most high tech hotel, with in-room delights such as electronically adjustable beds with massage settings, state of the art 46" full HD 3D televisions with complimentary 3D movies, surround sound, VoIP phones giving you low-cost telephone calls, a personal iPad through which you can also order room service, and a flat-screen television in the bathroom concealed behind steam-proof mirrors.

Wi-Fi: The Luxury Traveler's Friend?
A word of warning: don't anticipate that staying in a luxury hotel, even an expensive one, will provide you with free internet access. Unfortunately, all too often the opposite is true.

Wi-Fi rates can range from the derisory to the frankly outrageous – anything up to $15 an hour – and you'll usually find the highest rates at the most exclusive hotels and on cruise ships. On top of this, the service can be poor with drop-offs and slow connections. On a cruise ship this can be explained due to them using satellite connections, but in hotels, staff often apologize with "It's a common problem in the part of the hotel that you're staying in."

This is bad enough, but in this highly-connected age, when social media offers the opportunity to share our travel recommendations instantly, some hotels are doing guests and themselves a disservice.

If you want to avoid a hotel's fees, look out for shops and eateries that provide free Wi-Fi. Alternatively, if you really need internet throughout your stay, pick up a mobile Wi-Fi, or Mi-Fi, device which uses the local cellular network. You can find international ones or pick one up at your destination.

It's the Little Things that Count
Attention to detail defines the luxury experience. Yes, there are gourmet meals in Michelin-starred restaurants, treatments in underwater spas and the extravagance of hotel interiors adorned with gold leaf. But luxury travel providers realize that it's the little things that underline the experience and make luxury stand out from the crowd.

A five-star welcome at Thailand's Amari Orchid in Pattaya.

Every area of luxury travel has its little extras, from noise cancelling headphones on first class flights to luxury brand toiletries in hotels, and spa changing areas equipped with tiny essentials. But what else can you expect?

- Pillow menus – everything from hypo-allergenic to organic buckwheat hull fillings.
- In-room spa treatments.
- Butler service.
- In-room chefs – particularly in fractional properties, suites and penthouses.

In fact, you'll find that nothing is too much trouble in most luxury hotels, villas, cruises and more. If it hasn't been thought of already, just ask.

Choose Your Luxury Experience

By following the tips in section 2, Dream Trips to Real Trips, you will have liberated luxury and should now have extra money in your pocket. What will you do with it? Here are a few luxurious ideas you could indulge in on your trip.

- Enjoy a gourmet meal: the Michelin Guide lists the best restaurants in the world's major cities. Alternatively, ask your hotel for recommendations of renowned restaurants serving local food in your destination.

- Have dinner at the chef's table: as well as a fantastic meal, you will gain wonderful insights into the secrets of the world's best chefs.

- Take a helicopter ride: whether it's over a natural wonder like the Grand Canyon or a great city like New York, it's fabulous.

- Take to the skies in a hot air balloon: perhaps over the savannahs of Africa.

- Watch the sun set on a champagne cruise: we had one for our wedding in Thailand – it was spectacular.

- Learn to scuba dive: we've had a "try dive" and loved it so much that we're planning to learn.

- Grab some tickets: whether it's Broadway or a Madonna concert, it can be a great vacation memory.

- Soak up a spa day: whether it's at your hotel or a nearby spa, it can be the ultimate way to relax.

- Book tickets for a big sporting event: travel allows for some once in a lifetime events for sports fans.

- Charter a yacht for a day: take to the sea and go where you want and when. You could even try deep sea fishing.

An Ayurvedic Adventure

"Eat and nourish your soul," he said with quiet intensity. At the head of the table the elderly Ayurvedic doctor's wispy gray hair mingled with a Ho Chi Minh-like beard at his slim shoulders.

On the banana leaf before us a waiter placed small portions of colorful foods and juices. In traditional local fashion we ate with our hands.

> ❝ *I'd had some odd treatments, and this was certainly one of the most curious, but within minutes waves of relaxation transformed me into human Jell-O.* ❞

The meal was the second act in our Ayurvedic experience. Days before, Sarah and I had treated ourselves to the best massages of our lives at Poovar Island Resort, our four-star hotel on Kerala's idyllic backwaters. Having saved money on our trip, we decided to indulge, and discover this ancient system of Indian medicine, diet and lifestyle. Well, we thought we'd dip our toe with a massage at least.

Sarah was led to a room by a masseuse while a masseur took me to another.

There I sat naked on a small stool, while he took colored powder from a small bucket and placed it ritually over my body. Next I lay on a large green floor mat above which a rope hung from the ceiling. My masseur poured an enormous quantity of oil over me, took hold of the rope, balanced like a ballet dancer, and began massaging me with great dexterity with his right foot.

I'd had some odd treatments, and this was certainly one of the most curious, but within minutes waves of relaxation transformed me into human Jell-O.

I drifted off and though it seemed like only seconds later, some minutes passed. Then my masseur guided my oily body to a wooden bench with small sides to it. Although it seemed unnecessary, more oil was poured over me and the third stage of the massage began – this time by hand.

The copious amounts of oil made me gently slip and slide across the table, but soon I felt myself drifting in and out of sleep.

After 90 minutes of blissful relaxation it was over, except for an intensive shower to clean up the contented human oil slick I'd become.

Stepping Out into the Real World

From zooming through a fast-track security line to resting on a handmade ergonomic bed with rare Russian goose down pillows, luxury is wonderful. If your idea of heaven is sipping mojitos on a white sand beach for two weeks, that's ok – use the tips we've suggested to find a get-away-from-it-all break.

But for many, luxury is only part of the travel experience. After all, you won't discover the delight of meeting people and sharing their corner of the earth if you stay within the confines of your five-star hotel or on the sun deck of a cruise ship.

Hotel life is not real life, especially not when you compare the luxuries of a hotel with the harsh realities of life in a developing country. The perfectly dressed, attentive hotel staff may well go back to a crowded home with no running water or sewerage.

We don't raise these points to denigrate the luxury experience, but to suggest that getting out and seeing your destination will increase your understanding of it. Your world is only as small as you make it.

Luxury provides travelers with a comfortable base from which to venture forth and discover, as well as a pleasant place to unwind on days of pure relaxation. But if you're fascinated by a country's culture, history, and society, you'll certainly need to liberate yourself from your luxury hotel and step into real life. Here are our tips for having a real experience:

- Try setting out on foot to see your destination. It's at street level that you'll best appreciate the sights, smells, and sounds of the area.

- Take a taxi to see a specific attraction. In some countries you can negotiate very affordable fares with taxi drivers to drive you around for a day.

- Take a local bus or train. We're big fans of traveling by rail when abroad, as stations and trains are familiar yet different in each country, and bus journeys reveal a microcosm of local life.

Above: We hired a taxi driver, right, to take us from Chiang Mai to the Golden Triangle in northern Thailand for the day. He was able to take us to an authentic tea shop and to visit a Karen hill tribe in the region, below.

- Eat away from your hotel. Even if you're on an all-inclusive vacation, venture out at least one night to try local food at a restaurant or even sample good quality street food. Ask someone at the hotel or your taxi driver for their favorite place for lunch – not the tourist spot, but where they like to eat.

- Learn a few words of the local language and use them. Going to the effort of learning to say "hello," "yes," "no," "please," and "thank you," wherever you are, is always appreciated by locals.

- Combine a luxury stay with some form of voluntary work. Many hotels, glampsites, train and even cruise companies run sustainable tourism programs or host responsible tours to visit with indigenous communities. Alternatively, find out if there's an independent program close by. There are many ethical considerations involved with volunteering. Make sure that you are actually making a contribution and not taking work from a local.

- Try your hand at a creative workshop led by a local. Learn any number of skills from cooking to dancing, carving to weaving. It provides a great perspective on local culture.

Visitors to some countries – certain Caribbean islands, for example – are warned that the country beyond the gates of their hotel is not safe. Safety is a critical consideration, but unless there are specific warnings– at which point you must take all necessary precautions – we would certainly venture out.

Most importantly, have an exciting, enlightening, enriching and safe experience.

Sarah's Bangkok

As much as I enjoy a luxury hotel stay, for me the ultimate attraction is the destination. When I visit Bangkok, the capital of Thailand, I have an established routine, which encapsulates my desire to stay in luxury but delve into the beating heart of the city.

An Australian friend, Leisa, introduced me to two places that have become central to my visits to the city: Nancy's Beauty Salon (or, as I call it, the Pink Place, due to the girly pink signage and furnishings), and the nearby Wild Orchid Villa, in the backpacker quarter of the city around Khao San Road.

> ❝ *There I gaze upon bright Thai silks and ornate handicrafts cheek-by-jowl with washing machine parts, alien-looking plants, and pets.* ❞

At Nancy's I delight in having a facial, manicure, pedicure and Thai massage for less than $30. I could get the same in my five-star hotel, but it would cost ten times as much and I'd miss out on the fabulous local characters and flutter of people selling everything from fisherman trousers to deep fried insects, which are something of a local delicacy.

After my treatments I pop into the Wild Orchid, a cheap but very cheerful eatery, for my first taste of delectable Thai food: Phad Thai noodles or fried rice. Other nights I'll eat at some of the city's ubiquitous street food stalls where I point at what I want and revel in the rich complex flavors of Thai cuisine, or stop off at cafes where local workers gather to slurp soup from indelicate blue plastic bowls.

At the other end of the spectrum I like to visit some of Bangkok's premier hotels, such as the Mandarin Oriental for cocktails, or head up to the Banyan Tree Hotel's open-air Vertigo and Moon Bar on the 61st floor.

Retail therapy is also on the agenda at the chic air-conditioned malls of Siam Square, where Versace and Gucci catch my eye. And I can't resist shooting through the city aboard the Skytrain to Chatuchak Weekend Market. There I gaze upon bright Thai silks and ornate handicrafts cheek-by-jowl with washing machine parts, alien-looking plants, and pets. Or I head down to Chinatown to eye antique Oriental furniture.

Then, seeking calm in this cacophonous city, I head to Wat Pho, the Temple of the Reclining Buddha, to breathe in its quiet splendor.

It isn't just Bangkok. It's now my Bangkok, and I love it.

Sarah takes her mom to one of her favorite places in Bangkok, Wat Pho, the Temple of the Reclining Buddha.

❝ *Luxury travel is all about the moments and being inspired by them. Enjoying the cool droplets of mist on my face in the cloud forests of Monteverde. Sitting on a beach feeling the silky water of the sea lapping around my toes. Feasting my eyes on the colors of the lagoon in Bora Bora. Lying on the deck of a boat in the Whitsundays and staring at the Milky Way. Curling up in a five-star hotel bed. Catching the rich scent of a Pinotage as I swirl it in a glass. Savoring the wondrous texture and flavors of Italian ice-cream. Or discovering a little bit more about myself. These are my moments of luxury - my Velvet Escapes.* ❞

Keith Jenkins, VelvetEscape.com

PLAYING IT SAFE

"A journey is like marriage. The certain way to be wrong is to think you control it."

John Steinbeck,
*Travels with Charley:
In Search of America*

Words to the Wise: Consumer Rights

We have established ways in which you can liberate luxury, some of which are a little less than conventional. It's important, therefore, to know your rights as a consumer and ensure that you're covered if something goes wrong.

If you book with an agent, they will act on your behalf to see that restitution is made if you have a problem with part of your travel experience. If you book yourself, you will have to be your own advocate in the case of a problem.

Consumer laws vary in every country and it's advisable to understand your rights. In the US, for example, there's no specific protection for bookings made through tour operators or travel agencies. However, under the Fair Credit Billing Act, credit card customers have the right to refuse to pay charges for services not rendered.[35] There are also some passenger protections in the event of airline delays and cancellations as well as denied boarding.

The first place to go for help if things go wrong is the company that you purchased tickets from. An airline or tour operator may refer you back to your travel agent. Michael Cintron of the International Airline Passengers Association said: "For situations directly within an airline's control, such as finding you an alternate flight in the event of a cancellation, you'd go to the airline first. However, a ticket exchange or refund request will typically have you marching back to your booking agent."

However, the DIY traveler can mitigate certain risks by purchasing travel insurance that specifically covers events that most basic insurance won't, such as the sudden collapse of an airline in the middle of a vacation, which could leave passengers stranded and paying their own way home. If an insurance policy covers airline insolvency, you should be protected. Reading the fine print is key.

Avoiding Travel Scams

Sadly, there are a number of travel scams to which people fall prey. Here are some to look out for:

- Employ caution when dealing with holiday clubs, many of which will pass themselves off as legitimate timeshare businesses, claiming access to accommodation from large timeshare companies. This is not the case. Fully check the credentials of a holiday club, and determine whether they can deliver on their promises before purchasing a membership.

- Never give your credit card details out without knowing who you're dealing with. Watch out for situations such as a phone call in the middle of the night from someone claiming to work at the hotel's front desk, saying there's been a problem with your credit card. They may ask you to read the number back one more time, and then use your card details to steal from you. Instead of giving them your details, telephone the front desk yourself to verify the call.

- Always check the cost of a taxi journey before you head off; if the taxi is fitted with a meter, ask the driver to switch it on at the start of the journey if he doesn't do so automatically.

- Beware of booking anything with a credit card when using an unsecured Wi-Fi network.

- Don't fall for fake competitions. Fraudsters can contact you by phone or e-mail claiming that you've won a luxury vacation but need to pay a fee to secure it. This is a scam. You may win accommodation and have to pay for flights but should never have to pay a fee for a prize.

The Burj Khalifa – the world's tallest building is in Dubai, in the United Arab Emirates, traditionally one of the safest places in the Middle East and considered one of the world's premier luxury destinations.

Is Luxury Travel Safe?

The reality is that luxury, like most sectors of travel, is rarely marred by major incidents where tourists are specifically targeted. However, we feel it important to cover safety because many travelers believe that the more expensive the travel experience, the more protected they will be. This is not the case.

Over the years, there have been incidents of travelers being targeted. Sadly, tourists vacationing in resorts in the Caribbean have been robbed and murdered,[36] there have been bombings specifically targeting tourists in Bali,[37] and there have been terrorist atrocities such as the attacks on guests at hotels in Mumbai in 2008.[38]

With all these major incidents you'd be tempted to think that travel companies would be working hard to analyze risks, implement tightened security measures and ensure the safety of guests. Not so.

"Travel companies are not doing anything more to increase your safety," explained one of the world's leading authorities on tourism security, Dr Peter Tarlow, the president of Tourism and More, and a risk management consultant for Brazil's World Cup 2014 planning team. "Certain locations will. London upped its security ahead of the Olympics in 2012, but it always gets let go after the event."

Travelers might expect to find better security in five-star hotels or on cruise ships, but unfortunately there are as many incidents in five-star as in two- or three-star hotels. Hotel security is usually at its best when the city or country makes an issue of it and pressures them into action.

Tarlow points out that the travel business is run by marketers who know little about security and concern themselves with it even less.

Though this may be true, we can offer a little anecdotal evidence in support of the travel industry. At five-star hotels in Turkey, for example, there are barriers and security checkpoints at the end of long driveways. Our vehicles – invariably taxis – have also been checked with mirrors for bombs.

Though airport and airline security has been tightened to levels where passengers themselves can feel criminalized, the rest of the travel industry isn't so safety conscious. It is vital that luxury travelers are aware that they are as much, if not more, of a target for criminals as other passengers. You need to be proactive about your safety.

Seven Ways to Keep You and Your Belongings Safe

When traveling, ask yourself these questions: What are my risks and what are the dangers I'm facing? Have I done a good risk assessment?

Tarlow proposes the following tips to ensure happy and safe travels:

1. Don't flaunt your wealth or goods. If you can't afford to lose it – emotionally or economically – don't take it.

2. Make sure your luggage is as beaten up as possible. "Louis Vuitton luggage might as well say, 'Please come to my room and steal,'" Tarlow explained. Go to a department store, buy the brightest, ugliest case you can find, and throw it down the stairs a few times. The uglier it is the less likely people will see you as a prospect.

3. Dress according to the destination. Don't just conform to specific cultural or religious rules, but try to blend in.

4. Don't take too much cash with you – but don't go without any. Don't take many credit cards, but travel with more than one. Also, keep your wallet or purse on the side of your body furthest away from the street and always carry wallets in your front pocket, never the back. BONUS TIP: cross two rubber bands around your wallet and it can't be taken from your pocket by thieves.

5. Don't consider your hotel room a completely private and safe space. Everyone working there has access to it, and hotels do not carry out security analyses of staff.

6. Place your passport in the safe and carry a photocopy of it with you when out and about. If a police officer happens to stop you, you can show them the photocopy. They can always check the original later.

7. Room safes are not 100 percent safe, nor do hotels take responsibility for items removed from them. To ensure the safety of valuable items, ask reception to put them in the hotel's safety deposit box.

A Phantom Menace?

Let's take a slice of reality – in all the years that Terry and I have traveled together we've thankfully never experienced theft, attack or been close to a terrorist incident. And we hope and pray we never will.

> **❝** *We found ourselves at a lonely pier late at night, just us and a group of four young men, each looking us up and down, the air thick with collusion.* **❞**

There have been a few anxious moments – the kind when you know you've made a stupid decision - and one incident in Thailand is indelibly etched on our memories.

While staying in Railey Beach, Krabi, we had to get a water taxi to Ao Nang. The last one back to Railey Beach left early without warning because of unusually high tides, and we were literally left high and dry with no route back to our hotel, except via a tuk-tuk to the next pier.

We found ourselves at a lonely pier late at night, just us and a group of four young men, each looking us up and down, the air thick with collusion. It was strange, really. Our command of the Thai language was very limited, but we could tell something was going on. Long gone were the famed Thai smiles. And, when they did speak to us in English, there were searching, private questions: "Where are you staying?" "How much did it cost you?" "Do you have a lot of money?"

We were bracing ourselves for trouble. Terry was gripping the only weapon we had between us, a small Swiss Army knife he carried merely for the tiny flashlight attached to it to help us navigate paths in the dark. It really wasn't much at all, but it offered a crumb of defensive comfort.

We waited for thirty minutes for the boat operator to arrive, only to see him greet the other four men and join their surly huddle. Then we set off across a dark but now placid sea.

My mind swirled, convinced that we'd be attacked on the 15 minute journey to Railey. But as the boat set off, the tension and hostility eased. Reaching Railey, the most hostile of the men smirked as we got off the boat, and mumbled something in Thai.

Perhaps he'd wanted to rob us and his friends had backed out. Maybe they realized we were readying for a fight and decided not to risk it. It's even possible that they meant us no harm whatsoever. But it's rare for us to be so in tune and alert to danger in that way, both sensing the risk.

Either way, the experience made us more thoughtful and aware of danger when we travel, knowing that even when staying in a country where we feel 99 percent safe heading to and from our quality hotels, there's always a risk of crime.

Watch What You Eat: Tasty Tips

Fact: most buffets should come with a health warning.

Whether it's in a hotel, an all-inclusive resort or on a cruise ship, buffets can be breeding grounds for any number of bacteria. But there are many other risks to travelers from food and drink, such as traveler's diarrhea and the highly contagious norovirus (which can spread like wildfire on cruise ships).[39]

A few words of advice:

- Avoid buffets where food is kept in lukewarm pans, or has been exposed to flies.

- Avoid tap water in certain countries. As a general rule, you'll be safe in the US, Europe, and Australasia, but check tourist guides or ask hotel staff.

- As above, don't take ice in your drinks, or eat salad which may have been washed in water that is questionable.

- Select restaurants and street vendors that are busy and cook food fresh. A regular turnover of food will mean it's fresher.

- Avoid uncooked fruits and vegetables, unless they have thick skins that can be peeled.

- Avoid unpasteurized milk, cheese or ice cream.

- Wash your hands before every meal and/or use sanitizing hand gels or wipes, especially on cruise ships.

A cautionary note by way of Sarah's personal experience: never eat sushi before a 12-hour flight. As she discovered to her dismay, sushi, as delicious as it is, can easily be a source of immediate and violent food poisoning as it contains raw and cooked elements and is served at room temperature. Having eaten it before a flight from Bangkok to London, she endured an agonizing trip.

GO IN STYLE

"We live in a wonderful world that is full of beauty, charm and adventure. There is no end to the adventures we can have if only we seek them with our eyes open."

*Jawaharial Nehru,
first prime minister of India,
(1889-1964)*

More Luxury, More Choice

From Chichen Itza in Mexico, to Petra in Jordan, to Victoria Falls in Zambia, to the backwaters of Kerala in India, and onwards, we have explored the world and enjoyed luxury for less.

Our travels began as they do for most people - consulting with travel agents and accepting prices given. But, we realized it didn't have to be that way.

Instead, we liberated luxury. We saved money, traveled in style, had more vacations and, importantly, designed our vacations to our desires. Yes, an understated benefit of planning your own vacation is you get what you want. Wherever possible, you choose your departure date, airport, airline, length of stay, accommodation, and more. You don't have to settle for the airlines or hotels that a tour company packages for you.

We said in the opening chapters that luxury was about more, and we've shown you how to have not just more luxury, value and experiences, but more choice. You are not limited to what travel companies want to sell you. By perusing the full range of options, from traditional agents, to online travel booking sites, to flash sales and loyalty programs, you can create your own trip.

Plus, you will feel great in the process. Liberating luxury is satisfying, empowering and instills confidence. The more you save, the more satisfied you will feel; the more you book your own luxury travels, the more empowered you will become; and the more you travel, the more confident you will become.

In writing this book we wanted to share our knowledge gained over the past decade and to empower you to take control of your travel planning. By using our 12-point plans, you can liberate luxury, find fabulous deals and gain even more from your travels. So now it's your turn:

- Define your sense of luxury.

- Find ideas on our Luxury Travel page: livesharetravel.com/luxury-travel.

- Decide who can best deliver your trip and in which destination.

- Use our insider tips to plan and book your vacation.

- Put the money you've saved towards vacation extras.

- Decide if you want to extend your vacation with extra luxuries, such as helicopter flights or gourmet meals at top restaurants, or if you wish to put your savings towards another trip.

- Travel with confidence.

- Get out and see your destination and experience the local culture.

- Share your top luxury travel tips, stories and more with us at LiveShareTravel.com and on our Facebook page.

We've given you the insider tips and advice to liberate luxury. Now it's time to strike out and use the information to make the world your luxury oyster.

Light up your luxury travels. The Chedi, Oman.

Sarah & Terry Lee

We've brought together a number of travel websites, books, apps and resources to inspire your luxury travels, and help you plan and book your flights, accommodation, and more. You'll also find information here on the tools we find useful while on the road. But as we could write a book on travel resources alone, head on over to *The Luxury Traveler's Handbook* online resource page to discover more *livesharetravel.com/luxury-travel*.

Books
Other Traveler's Handbooks
The Career Break Traveler's Handbook, by Jeff Jung
The Food Traveler's Handbook, by Jodi Ettenberg
The Solo Traveler's Handbook, by Janice Waugh
The Volunteer Traveler's Handbook, by Shannon O'Donnell

Destination Guides
The major publishers of destination guides – Frommer's, Lonely Planet, Rough Guides, and Fodor's for example, have much of the world covered and offer a good general guide to a place. But there are some guidebooks that focus on luxury travel:

Hg2 A Hedonist's Guide has 48 guide books and iPhone apps to cities and ski resorts around the world, as well as foodie guides to London and New York: hg2.com/stores.

Wallpaper* City Guides and iPhone apps cover 80 urban destinations around the world: phaidon.com/store/travel.

Travel Apps
We love Lifehacker.com's daily lists of apps (they don't just cover travel, but are very useful). Here are some great travel apps for iPhone and Android.

For Inspiration
ArounderTouch.com
FourSquare.com
Instagram.com
Stay City Guides: stay.com/mobile
Tripwolf.com
Yelp: yelp.co.uk/yelpmobile

Tools for Travel
Evernote: an excellent note taking app: evernote.com/download.

iTranslate+ on iPhone or iTranslatePro on Android. Also iTranslate Voice for voice translations: sonicomobile.com.

Packing (+TO DO): a great app for packing and pre-travel to-do lists: quinnscape.com.

Skype: plainly and simply one of the best ways to stay in touch with home: skype.com.

TripIt Pro: email your travel information to this app and it organizes your trip itinerary for you. It will also alert you of gate changes for your flight: tripit.com/uhp/mobile.

Wi-Fi Finder: as the name suggests, this app helps you find hotspots nearby: jiwire.com/iphone, and jiwire.com/android.

Word Lens: ever wanted to translate a menu? Scan it with Word Lens and it will do the hard work for you: questvisual.com/us.

Luxury Travel Blogs
ALuxuryTravelBlog.com
JustLuxe.com/travel
LuxuryTravelBible.com

LuxuryTravelMom.com
MrsOAroundTheWorld.com
PerfectBoutiqueHotel.com
SimplyLuxuryTravel.com
TheCoolhunter.co.uk/travel
VelvetEscape.com

Planning Tools

Google Earth: google.com/earth/index.html Get an aerial view of your destination from the comfort of your home.

Google Maps Street View: maps.google.com/help/maps/streetview is a good tool for getting a street-level perspective of your destination.

SeatGuru.com: an airline review site and has cabin maps to show you the best and worst seats on your airline/aircraft.

TripAdvisor.com: Traveler's reviews of accommodation, attractions and more.

XE.com: currency converter

Flash Sales

Bloomspot.com/Travel
Groupenture.com (for activity-driven vacations)
Groupon: groupon.com/getaways
Jetsetter.com
LivingSocial.com
Mind Body Green: travel.mindbodygreen.com (yoga retreats and eco-resorts)
OverstockVacations.com
SecretEscapes.com
SniqueAway.com
Spire.com

Travelzoo.com
TripAlertz.com
Vacationist.com
Voyage-Prive.com

Hack Your Way to Luxury

Follow the travel hackers' rules to travel and you could net yourself some stylish savings. Travel hackers spend a huge amount of time researching ways to game loyalty programs and find ways to travel cheaply in style. These sites are some useful resources:

AwardWallet.com
FlyerTalk.com
FrugalTravelGuy.com
HelpMeTravelCheap.Com
MilePoint.com
ThePointsGuy.com
TravelHacking.org

Loyalty Programs

United Airlines: united.com/web/en-US/content/mileageplus/default.aspx
Hilton HHonors: hhonors1.hilton.com
Hyatt: hyatt.com/hyatt/about/our-company/hyatt-gold-passport.jsp
Oneworld: oneworld.com/ffp
SkyTeam: skyteam.com/en/Why-SkyTeam/Frequent-Flyer-Program
Starwood Cash & Points: starwoodhotels.com/preferredguest
Virgin Atlantic: virgin-atlantic.com/en/us/frequentflyer/index.jsp

DIY-Packaging
Flight Price Comparison Sites
These sites provide an overview of flight prices from all airlines in one place.

Cheapflights.com
CheapOAir.com
FareCompare.com
Fly.com
Hipmunk.com
Momondo.com
Skyscanner.com
Orbitz.com

Book flights, Accommodation and More with the Sites Below
Ebookers.com
Expedia.com
Hipmunk.com
Kayak.com
Lastminute.com
Opodo.co.uk
Orbitz.com
Travelocity.com
TravelRepublic.co.uk
TravelSupermarket.com

Hotel Booking and Price Comparison Sites
Agoda.com
Booking.com
Hotels.com
LateRooms.com
Octopus.com
Room77.com
Trivago.com
Venere.com

Where to Stay

This is by no means a complete list of accommodation brands around the world, but highlights some of those mentioned in *The Luxury Traveler's Handbook*.

Hotels and Hotel Brands

968parkhotel.com
Atlantis.com
Bahia-Principe.com
BanyanTree.com
Beaches.com
BuccamentBay.com
Burj Al Arab: jumeirah.com
FourSeasons.com
HaciendaTresRios.com
Hilton.com
Hyatt.com
Intercontinental.com
LuxuryFamilyHotels.co.uk
MandarinOriental.com
Marriott.com
MorgansHotel.co.uk

OneAndOnlyResorts.com
PoovarIslandResort.com
Raffles.com
RedCarnationHotels.com
RelaisChateaux.com
ShaWellnessClinic.com
Sheraton: starwoodhotels.com/sheraton
Small Luxury Hotels of the World: slh.com
The Ritz: theritzlondon.com
The Savoy: fairmont.com
TheBodyHoliday.com
ThePlaza.com
ThePrivilegeFloor.com
W Hotels: starwoodhotels.com/whotels
Westin: starwoodhotels.com/westin

Apartments and Socially-Sourced Accommodation

Airbnb.com
FlipKey.com
Housetrip.com
Onefinestay.com
Roomorama.com
Wimdu.com

Vacation Ownership Accommodation
ArcosGardens.com
Disney Vacation Club: disneyvacationclub.disney.go.com
Fairmont Heritage Place/Residences: fairmont.com/explore/residences
Four Seasons Residences: residences.fourseasons.com
HiltonGrandVacationsClub.com
MarriottVacationClub.com
RitzCarltonClub.com

Timeshare and Fractional Exchange Companies
DialAnExchange.com
IntervalWorld.com
RCI.com
TheRegistryCollection.com
eXpectations.com

Timeshare Rentals
Endless Vacation Rentals: endless-vacation-rentals.com

Timeshare Resales
Worldwide Timeshare Hypermarket: timeshare-hypermarket.com

Villas
AbercrombieKent.com has villa rentals around the world.
Wimco.com specializes in the Caribbean.
VillasOfDistinction.com has more than 2,500 villas in the Caribbean, Europe, Mexico, and the US.
VillaEurope.com has 550 properties in Italy and England.
VillaLuxe.com has 500 villas in the Caribbean, Mexico, and Costa Rica.

Glamping Accommodation
4 Rivers Floating Lodge: ecolodges.asia
MinaretStation.com

Cruise Companies

Carnival.com
CelebrityCruises.com
CostaCruises.com
Cunard.com
Disney Cruises: DisneyCruise.disney.go.com
HollandAmerica.com
MSCCruises.com
Norwegian Cruise Lines: ncl.com
P&O Cruises: pocruises.com
Princess.com
Regent Seven Seas: rssc.com
RoyalCaribbean.com
Seabourn.com
Seadream.com
SilverSea.com
StarClippers.com

River Cruises

AmaWaterways.com
Uniworld.com
VikingRiverCruises.com

Luxury Trains

BlueTrain.com
ElTranscantábricoClasico.com
GreatSouthernRail.com
Orient-Express.com
Maharajas' Express: maharajas-express-india.com
RockyMountaineer.com
Rovos.com

Luxury Volunteer Programs

Ritz-Carlton Give Back Getaways: corporate.ritzcarlton.com/en/about/givebackgetaways.htm has programs around the world.

SandalsFoundation.org is operated by the Sandals group of resorts with volunteer opportunities in the Caribbean.

Creative Travel

CreativeTourismNetwork.org: creative trips in destinations such as Barcelona. CreativeParis.info for artistic activities in the French capital.

Kreativ Reisen Österreich kreativreisen.at organizes creative travel tours in Austria, in German and English.

Luxury Travel Extras

Airport Parking
MeteorMeetAndGreet.com

Airport Lounges
PriorityPass.com has various membership plans which give you lounge access around the world.

Airport-Hotel Transfers
WorldAirportTransfer.com

Resorthoppa.com

Car Rental
Alamo.com

Avis.com

EuropCar.com

Hertz.com

International Mobile Internet (Mi-Fi) suppliers
CellularAbroad.com

XComGlobal.com

Government Travel Advisories

Canada: voyage.gc.ca/countries_pays/menu-eng.asp
US: travel.state.gov/travel/cis_pa_tw/tw/tw_1764.html

Visa Information

For Australian Citizens: dfat.gov.au/visas/index.html
For Canadian Citizens: voyage.gc.ca/index-eng.asp
For US Citizens: travel.state.gov/travel/travel_1744.html

The Luxury List

You can find travel companies highlighted as being at the top of their game in the following annual listings:

Condé Nast Traveler's Gold Awards and Readers' Choice Awards: cntraveller.com/awards
The Skytrax World Airline Awards: worldairlineawards.com
The TripAdvisor Travelers' Choice Awards: tripadvisor.com/TravelersChoice
World Travel Awards: worldtravelawards.com

Artist Elisabeth Holzschuster taught Terry to capture the Austrian countryside in oil paints on a creative travel trip with Kreativ Reisen.

Endnotes

[1] Horwath HTL for International Luxury Travel Market. The Future of Luxury Travel, iltm.net/files/the_future_of_luxury_travel_report.pdf, June 2011.

[2] "The Platinum Circle" Condé Nast Traveler, cntraveler.com/gold-list/2012/platinum-circle#slide=1

[3] "The Platinum Circle: Africa & The Middle East" Condé Nast Traveler, cntraveler.com/gold-list/2012/platinum-circle#slide=199

[4] "The Platinum Circle: Africa & The Middle East" Condé Nast Traveler, cntraveler.com/gold-list/2012/platinum-circle#slide=207

[5] "The Platinum Circle: Asia, Australia & The Pacific" Condé Nast Traveler, cntraveler.com/gold-list/2012/platinum-circle#slide=185

[6] "The Platinum Circle: Africa & The Middle East" Condé Nast Traveler, cntraveler.com/gold-list/2012/platinum-circle#slide=195

[7] "The Platinum Circle: Asia, Australia & The Pacific" Condé Nast Traveler, cntraveler.com/gold-list/2012/platinum-circle#slide=179

[8] "The Platinum Circle: The Americas" Condé Nast Traveler, cntraveler.com/gold-list/2012/platinum-circle#slide=150

[9] "The Platinum Circle: Europe" Condé Nast Traveler, cntraveler.com/gold-list/2012/platinum-circle#slide=43

[10] "The Platinum Circle: Asia, Australia & The Pacific" Condé Nast Traveler, cntraveler.com/gold-list/2012/platinum-circle#slide=174

[11] "The Platinum Circle: Africa & The Middle East" Condé Nast Traveler, cntraveler.com/gold-list/2012/platinum-circle#slide=204

¹²"The Platinum Circle: Africa & The Middle East," Condé Nast Traveler, cntraveler.com/gold-list/2012/platinum-circle#slide=206

¹³"Rooms & Rates," The Privilege Floor gc.synxis.com/rez.aspx?Hotel=55891&Chain=8901&template=PrivilegeFloorHotelSR&shell=The-Privilege-Floor

¹⁴"Caribbean's Most Expensive All-Inclusive Resort Located in St Vincent," All Inclusive Resorts, allinclusiveresorts.net/press/luxury-resorts-2012.html, (February 28, 2012)

¹⁵"History of Boutique Hotels," USA Today, traveltips.usatoday.com/history-boutique-hotels-21480.html

¹⁶"Timeshare Basics from TimeSharing Today," TimeSharing Today, tstoday.com/members/timesharebasics.pdf

¹⁷"Tahoe's Green Hotel," 968 Park Spa Resort, 968parkhotel.com/green_tahoe_hotel

¹⁸"Home," The BodyHoliday, thebodyholiday.com

¹⁹"About SHA," The SHA Wellness Clinic, shawellnessclinic.com/about-sha

²⁰"SHA Diet," The SHA Wellness Clinic, shawellnessclinic.com/cuisine/sha-diet

²¹"Cruise Ships Orderbook," Cyber Cruises, cybercruises.com/orderbook.htm

²²Susan Heller, "Getting the Show on the Road," The New York Times, nytimes.com/1987/03/29/travel/getting-the-show-on-the-road.html?pagewanted=all&src=pm (March 29, 1987)

²³"Premium Economy Explained and Compared," SeatGuru, seatguru.com/charts/premium_economy.php

[24] "Long-haul Business Class Explained and Compared," SeatGuru, seatguru.com/charts/longhaul_business_class.php

[25] "Long-haul First Class Explained and Compared," SeatGuru, seatguru.com/charts/longhaul_first_class.php

[26] Molly McCluskey, "When Using a Travel Agent Can Save You Money," Daily Finance, dailyfinance.com/2012/06/21/when-using-a-travel-agent-can-save-you-money (June 21, 2012)

[27] Ypartnership (now MMGY Global), Portrait of American Travelers 2010, (2010)

[28] PhoCusWright, Travel's Daily Deal: Distribution Disruption or Flash in the Pan? (April 2012)

[29] Brian Kelly, "My Ranking of Airline Frequent Flyer Programs," The Points Guy, October 24, 2011, thepointsguy.com/2011/10/my-ranking-of-airline-frequent-flyer-programs

[30] "Fair Credit Billing," Federal Trade Commission, ftc.gov/bcp/edu/pubs/consumer/credit/cre16.shtm

[31] Horwath HTL for International Luxury Travel Market. The Future of Luxury Travel, iltm.net/files/the_future_of_luxury_travel_report.pdf, June 2011

[32] Jools Stone, "How to dress for the Orient-Express?", Trains on the Brain, November 2, 2011, trainsonthebrain.com/2011/11/02/how-to-dress-for-the-orient-express

[33] "Is there a dress code on board?", Cunard, ask.cunard.com/help/cunard/life-on-board/dress_code

[34] "Star Ratings (hotel class)," Expedia, expedia.com/Hotel-Star-Rating-Information

[35] "Credit and Your Consumer Rights," Federal Trade Commission, ftc.gov/bcp/edu/pubs/consumer/credit/cre01.shtm

[36] "Mullany Honeymoon Murders Hit Caribbean Paradise," Roger Pinney, BBC News, bbc.co.uk/news/uk-wales-14218970, (July 28, 2011)

[37] "Bali Terror Attack," BBC News, news.bbc.co.uk/2/hi/in_depth/asia_pacific/2002/bali/default.stm, (March 5, 2009)

[38] "Mumbai attacks," BBC News, news.bbc.co.uk/2/hi/in_depth/south_asia/2008/mumbai_attacks/default.stm (October 18, 2010)

[39] "Norovirus – What You Need to Know," Cruise Critic, cruisecritic.com/articles.cfm?ID=71

Sarah & Terry Lee

Sarah and Terry Lee are dedicated travelers and co-publishers of *LiveShareTravel.com* an online luxury travel and lifestyle magazine.

They love to bring luxury to their trips, traveling with the motto: "if you're on vacation then you may as well do it in style".

Sarah is a journalist and editor with more years experience than she likes to admit to, and is a member of the British Guild of Travel Writers. She has been mixing business with pleasure for many years, previously as managing editor on two travel magazines and more recently as publisher of LiveShareTravel.

Terry has worked in a variety of communications roles, most recently in travel marketing.

From America to India and Austria to South Africa they travel the world, reveling in the excitement and beauty of our wondrous planet. When they are at home, Sarah and Terry live in a little village in the heart of the English countryside.

Sarah & Terry Lee

The Luxury Traveler's Handbook

Sarah & Terry Lee

www.ingramcontent.com/pod-product-compliance
Lightning Source LLC
Chambersburg PA
CBHW041218070526
44584CB00001B/7